DATE DUE

THE INVISIBLE TENT

FORD MADOX FORD
Drawing by Mary S. Gordon

THE INVISIBLE TENT

The War Novels of Ford Madox Ford

BY AMBROSE GORDON, JR.

UNIVERSITY OF TEXAS PRESS AUSTIN

Library of Congress Catalog Card No. 64–22389

Printed in the United States of America
by the University of Texas Printing Division, Austin
Bound by Universal Bookbindery, Inc., San Antonio

FOR MARY

Preface

The war novels of Ford Madox Ford are, first of all, the tetralogy *Parade's End*: *Some Do Not, No More Parades, A Man Could Stand Up,* and *The Last Post.* But are they war novels? Surely not in the familiar sense, not in the way Dos Passos' *Three Soldiers* or Aldington's *Death of a Hero* or Mailer's *The Naked and the Dead* are war novels. But they are, and splendidly, novels about war, which means that they are also novels about peace. Earlier, Ford Madox Ford wrote two others: *The Marsden Case,* which is a novel but only indirectly about war, and *No Enemy* (published after the success of the tetralogy), about war but only indirectly a novel. I also include in this company *The Good Soldier*, a book that at first may seem quite out of place here. These are, I believe, Ford's masterpieces—some more than others. They form the subject of the present investigation.

Recently four full-scale studies of Ford's novels have appeared, and it might seem that the neglected master is already enjoying a certain boom. The boom is probably illusory. It is largely academic, an affair of the graduate schools. Within the past decade less than a half dozen of Ford's more than seventy books have been in print in the United States, and until very recently only two of these have been novels. Yet they are the right two. Placed beside *The Good Soldier* or *Parade's End,* most of his other works of fiction are nothing, a sad truth that a study of Ford's *oeuvre* is apt to minimize. Necessarily also such studies are somewhat generalizing and abstracted, since they represent the long view—*Parade's End* alone runs to over eight hundred pages and yet is only a fraction of the whole. In taking the long view a critic leaves out much, and sometimes what is left out seems to be nearly everything.

What follows, then, is to be a comparatively leisurely look at seven books (or four, depending on how one reckons *Parade's End*) written by Ford between the approach of World War I and the ending of the nineteen-twenties. Individual passages are quoted extensively and sometimes closely examined—a method familiar enough in the study of poetry. Ford asked for no less. Besides, there is no other way to maintain contact with the books themselves. An acute (though possibly not too modest) critic of the novel once said: "Our critical faculty may be admirable; we may be thoroughly capable of judging a book justly, if only we could watch it at ease. But fine taste and keen perception are of no use if we cannot retain the image of the book; and the image escapes and evades us like a cloud."

The difficulty of trying to see *Parade's End* and *The Good Soldier* too exclusively in the context of the total output, as Ford's recent students sometimes have, seems to me the danger of immersion: from that bath they may not come up alive again, they may be almost indistinguishably merged in the surrounding element. Ford was particularly anxious that this not happen, and I think he was telling no less than the truth when he said, in his Dedicatory Letter to *The Good Soldier*:

> Until I sat down to write this book—on the 17th of December, 1913—I had never attempted to extend myself, to use a phrase of race-horse training. . . . I had never really tried to put into any novel of mine *all* that I knew about writing. I had written rather desultorily a number of books—a great number—but they had all been in the nature of *pastiches*, of pieces of rather precious writing, or of *tours de force*. But I have always been mad about writing—about the way writing should be done and partly alone, partly with the companionship of Conrad, I had even at that date made exhaustive studies into how words should be handled and novels constructed.

To the extent that the "exhaustive studies" paid off in *The Good Soldier* and in *Parade's End*, Ford's earlier writing is probably recapitulated in them, is present like those gills in the human embryo or like the buried foundations of an older house. In what follows we shall examine various levels—or not so much "levels" as various strands of implication leading back from the master work to the long-protracted juvenilia. Yet ultimately fine novels contain their matrix within themselves.

Parts of this study have appeared previously in the *Sewanee Review*, *Modern Fiction Studies*, *Texas Studies in Literature and Language*, and The University of Texas student literary magazine *Riata*. They are here reprinted with grateful acknowledgment to the editors of these journals.

To Ford's literary executrix, Miss Janice Biala, I am indebted for generous permission to quote from the following books: *Between St. Dennis and St. George*, *No Enemy*, *The Marsden Case*, *Joseph Conrad: A Personal Remembrance*, *Return to Yesterday*, *It Was the Nightingale*, and *The March to Literature*. My thanks also go to Houghton Mifflin Company for permission to quote from *Portraits from Life*, and to the estate of Ford Madox Ford and to Alfred A. Knopf, Inc., for permission to quote from *The Good Soldier* and *Parade's End*.

Contents

THE INVISIBLE TENT

I used to think that, once out there, we should be surrounded by a magic and invisible tent that would keep from us all temporal cares. But we are not so surrounded, and it is not like that. The one nail does not knock out the other. There is that never ceasing waiting about; and the cold; and the long depressions. Now and then there is terrible noise—wearing, lasting for days. And some pain. All that is bearable. But what is desolating, what is beyond everything hateful, is that, round your transparent tent, the old evils . . . are unceasingly at work.

—*The Marsden Case*

i. A DIAMOND OF PATTERN

It moved and moved, under your eyes dissolving, yet always there. As if you should try to follow one diamond of pattern in the coil of an immense snake that was in irrevocable motion.

—*No More Parades*

How we find any writer is so often a matter of where we first came in—of how we first encountered him, with what expectations and hopes. In the case of Ford Madox Ford there are over sixty wrong places for a first encounter and there is perhaps only one right one, since, as Ford knew, first impressions stick. The beginning reader should probably not begin with "This is the saddest story I have ever heard." Nor even with "The two young men—they were of the English public official class—sat in the perfectly appointed railway carriage." There is a better spot than either of these—another window that opens onto more of the garden.

Here as elsewhere, chance has something to be said for it as a guide. It offered perhaps actually a slight advantage back when the novels that make up *Parade's End* were as yet uncollected and when *The Good Soldier* was still out of print and hard to come by. One then read what came his way, hit or miss, and with a minimum of prejudice. The official opening of *Parade's End*, the first scene of *Some Do Not*, lies suspiciously close to cliché: the two unnamed gentlemen who are found sitting in the elegant railway "carriage" just pulling out of the station. Its Edwardian prose is right but not arresting. And, in the collected reissue, the thickness of the volume lying in wait (836 pages) may give the reader pause. Besides, he has probably just finished considering Robie Macauley's Introduction, which announces that this novel's subject is "the last Tory," and he may have decided that he is not much interested in Tories, first or last.

But if the reader was so fortunate as to come to Ford deviously, by way of chance references to "Hueffer," picking up *It was the Nightingale* overseas and later forgetting most of it except for a strange anecdote about a dung beetle and a Corsican bandit, and another about a lone man making a stew, to be followed considerably later by Ford's little book on the English novel with its brave defiance and the occasional howlers (Ford talks about the personal friendship between Caxton and Chaucer), and if he came finally upon *No More Parades*, simply because the title was attractive, and with no knowledge of its subject or its relation to the other novels in the tetralogy—never having heard of Tietjens—then its opening page produces for him the true shock of recognition as it places him in a familiar, stiff, square, resonant, and (oddly) *brown* world. *No More Parades* opens with the words: "When you came in the space was desultory, rectangular, warm after the drip of the winter night, and transfused with a brown-orange dust that was light. It was shaped like the house a child draws."[1]

The scene is a hut in a replacement depot in France; the time is World War I. Outside there is an air raid going on. The brown light comes from "a bucket pierced with holes, filled with incandescent coke"; there is a gleam of brass in the background, two officers; two men squat by the brazier ("as if hierarchically smaller"); at one end of the hut two noncommissioned officers droop over tables "in attitudes of extreme indifference." The only sound is the murmur of the two men by the glowing bucket—they had been miners—talking "in a low sing-song of dialect, hardly audible," and the dripping from the eaves of the hut. But the brown light soon is irradiated by brighter colors.

An immense tea-tray, august, its voice filling the black circle of the horizon, thundered to the ground. Numerous pieces of sheet-iron said, "Pack. Pack. Pack." In a minute the clay floor of the hut shook, the drums of ears were pressed inwards, solid noise showered about the universe, enor-

[1] Ford Madox Ford, *Parade's End* (1950), p. 291. Subsequent page references will be to this edition.

mous echoes pushed these men—to the right, to the left, or down towards the tables, and crackling like that of flames among vast underwood became the settled condition of the night. Catching the light from the brazier as the head leaned over, the lips of one of the two men on the floor were incredibly red and full and went on talking and talking. (p. 291)

We catch the true Fordian note from the start. The prose is the quietest and suavest imaginable; to render noise the writer need not become noisy. Ford does not shout at us; rather, he is asking us to "contemplate" noise—battle noise. The tone is composed and the prose is composed; the noise is orchestrated for us. Two conversations are counterpointed: that of the miner and his comrade who went on talking; that of the immense tea-tray with the august voice, to which the numerous pieces of sheet iron replied, "Pack. Pack. Pack." The note of insanity and horror is all in one detail, the lips that were "incredibly red and full and went on talking and talking." Ford once said that the tone he sought in his prose was that of one English gentleman whispering into the ear of another English gentleman. The miners here, to be sure, are not gentlemen, quiet though they may be. And of H. M. officers one is crazy and is soon roaring: "He began to talk, faster than ever, about a circle. When its circumference came whole by the disintegration of the atom the world would come to an end" (p. 295). Here we are given a glimpse of violence in a matrix of quietness, of intimacy being violated by more than sound. *No More Parades* opens brownly upon a world in which gentlemen, alas, will no longer whisper.

The four Tietjens novels were written and published between 1924 and 1928 but were not brought together until a quarter of a century later. The collective title is Ford's (though there is some doubt as to whether he wished to include *The Last Post*). *Parade's End* is concerned with the relations between Christopher Tietjens, a mathematical genius and staunch Yorkshire squire, his estranged wife Sylvia, and a young suffragette named Valentine Wannop. There are in addition Tietjens' godfather General Campion, under whom he will later serve, a mad Pre-Raphaelite clergyman famous for his breakfasts, an Irish priest, Sylvia's mother, Tietjens' brother Mark, and some other memorable lesser characters. Tietjens, before his marriage to his future wife, had slept with her on a train; later when a child was born he learned that she did not know whether he was its father. They became increasingly estranged. *Some Do Not* introduces us to these characters a year or more before the outbreak of World War I and shows them later at war, with Tietjens home on sick leave. In *No More Parades*, Tietjens—as we have seen—is back in France serving in a giant replacement depot. Into this already chaotic scene his erring wife erupts, creating embarrassments and added confusion. The later volumes take him to the front (where Sylvia cannot get at him) and then bring him home again.

When the four novels appeared together in 1950 as *Parade's End* they were widely—and on the whole favorably—reviewed. But the reviewers seemed preoccupied with the peacetime, or civilian, sections of the book. No one appeared to be much interested in the war. Mr. Macauley in his Introduction defined *Parade's End* as a social history of a prophetic sort, explaining that England had for decades been slipping, the old social order was corrupted, *noblesse* no longer obliged; the war was merely the *coup de grâce* for a moribund society. And when Ford had said that his tetralogy was a war book—as he had—he was (Mr. Macauley's words) "hoaxing us." Some of the reviewers discussed the novel's formal qualities and all, of course, its content. But no one seemed much concerned about where the two meet—in the unique angle of vision that danger, and especially war, creates. Or perhaps it would be better to say in the unique quality of vision, all that takes place under brown light.

Ford himself was in no doubt about his subject: it was war, and *No More Parades* was the germinal volume. In much the way that Strether's conversation with little Bilham in the garden was the nub from which *The Ambassadors* grew, Tietjens' monologue to distract the mad McKechnie contains the germ for *Parade's End*. In that monologue he tells how at the beginning of the war he visited the War Office, where he found someone devising the ceremonial for the disbanding of a Kitchener battalion:

> You can't say we were not prepared in one matter at least. . . . Well, the end of the show was to be: the adjutant would stand the battalion at ease: the band would play *Land of Hope and Glory*, and then the adjutant would say: *There will be no more parades. . . .* Don't you see how symbolical it was: the band playing *Land of Hope and Glory*, and then the adjutant say-

ing *There will be no more parades?* . . . For there won't. There won't, there damn well won't. . . . No more Hope, no more Glory, no more parades for you and me any more. Nor for the country . . . Nor for the world, I dare say . . . None . . . Gone . . . Na poo, finny! No . . . more . . . parades! (pp. 306–307)

Ford's account of how his tetralogy was conceived is given in the autobiographical *It Was the Nightingale*, where we find him in postwar retirement—a sort of Cincinnatus-Henry James tending pigs:

I was covered with mud to the eyes, in old khakis, shorts and an old khaki army shirt. . . .

A voice said over the hedge:

"Didn't I once meet you at Henry James's?"

Standing above me on the bank was the comfortable and distinguished figure of Sir Edward Elgar. I did not remember having met him at Henry James's but I knew him for the local great man—and of course as the composer of the *Dream of Gerontius*—and *Land of Hope and Glory*.

There came into my mind suddenly the words: "The band will play: '*Land of Hope and Glory*' . . . The adjutant will say: 'There will be no more parades . . .' "

It worried me slightly that I could no longer be certain of all the phrases of that ceremonial for the disbanding of a battalion. . . . Nothing in the world was further from my thoughts than writing about the late war. But I suppose the idea was somewhere in my own subconscious, for I said to myself:

"If I do not do something about it soon it is possible I shall forget about the details. . . ." And I wondered how the common friend of myself and Sir Edward would have treated that intractable subject. I imagined the tortuous mind getting to work, the New England scrupulousness, the terrific involutions . . . and for the rest of the day and for several days more I lost myself in working out an imaginary war-novel on the lines of "What Maisie Knew."[2]

I found I still had by heart all the paragraphs of King's Regulations and Military Law that a regimental officer could be required to know. I went over in my mind every contour of the road from Bailleul to Locre, Locre-Pont de Nieppe, Nieppe down to Armentières—and of all the by-roads from Nieppe to Ploegsteert, Westoutre, Dramoutre. And I found that I could remember with astonishing vividness every house left, in Septem-

[2] Ford Madox Ford, *It Was the Nightingale* (1933), pp. 161–162.

ber 1916, along the whole road, and almost every tree—and hundreds of shell holes![3]

The contours, be it noted, came first; the primary motive of Ford's war novel was scenic—an assertion that may appear improbable to the reader who still thinks of the novelist's trade as "storytelling" or to the other, perhaps more sophisticated, reader who looks at every novel as symbolic action. Tietjens, Sylvia, Valentine Wannop, General Campion and the rest—their whole complex, funny, and sad imbroglio, and *Parade's End's* originality of form and style—all exist ultimately in order that Ford may penetrate and encompass that torn scene and re-create the particular kind of countryside that is called a battlefield. Tietjens' long parade begins and ends in a landscape.

In structure *Parade's End* is a strictly scenic novel. There is no general narrative: we are always locked in a particular scene, but the scene in turn is locked in a particular mind. It is a worrying mind, both anticipatory and mnemonic, since fragments of a remembered past and a looked-forward-to future are continually being filtered in. Henry James in his Preface to *The Awkward Age* explained the advantages he felt would accrue to the novelist who restricted himself as nearly as possible to the conventions of the stage play. However, Ford's affinities are more with the movies; his way of building up a scene—out of fragmented details, sudden "cuttings," shifts in "camera angle"—closely resembles film montage. As a result we are even more *in* the scene than James would have us—we are shut in, boxed in. In the opening scene of *No More Parades* its indoor—even domestic—aspects are stressed almost to the point of claustrophobia. About all the doings in that hut clings a suggestion of a monstrous tea party. The falling, and lethal, insides of shrapnel shells are called "candlesticks." Of the men by the brazier, one is muttering dejectedly about his unfaithful wife, another about a queer cow that "took a hatred for its cawve (up behind Caerphilly on the mountains)." The Canadian sergeant-major is worrying himself about a new pocketbook. The hut is shaped like the house a child draws. Inside is a curious air of false domesticity, into which the sounds of the outside come, appropriately, like the falling of a large tea-tray.

[3] *Ibid.*, pp. 224–225.

Ford's depiction of soldiers under fire is (or should have been) the death of a noble cliché: war seen as outdoors living, active, virile. There is much cold, much wet, much mud in his landscape, but there is very little action. Ford knew that war was mostly waiting. He also knew that in war one is always surrounded—if not by the enemy (please God!), then by one's own side. Tietjens finds himself in a hut, in a depot, in an army, on a front, in a war—and in a whole cluster of tangled social situations, his own and others'. Outside, forward and beyond, is what? Unknown. Meanwhile, there is the waiting. Wait long enough and it will come. But when the outside does come in, when Death enters the hut, his appearance and manners are strangely domesticated and prove to be in keeping with the scene.

The air raid has temporarily let up, the two runners have been sent out to see about candles and chow; but before long the planes return. More waiting. One runner re-enters with candles. There is now more light; the stage is set for someone's grand entrance. More talk takes place between the two officers, the younger becoming calmer—it is no longer his scene. As the elder officer (Tietjens) relaxes, his eyes play tricks on him. He has a piercing vision of his wife, "in a sheath gown of gold tissue, all illuminated, and her mass of hair, like gold tissue too, coiled round and round in plaits over her ears. The features very clean-cut and thinnish; the teeth white and small; the breasts small; the arms thin, long and at attention at her sides" (p. 299). More waiting. Then:

> A man, brown, stiff, with a haughty parade step, burst into the light. He said with a high wooden voice:
>
> " 'Ere's another bloomin' casualty." In the shadow he appeared to have draped half his face and the right side of his breast with crape. He gave a high, rattling laugh. He bent, as if in a stiff bow, woodenly at his thighs. He pitched, still bent, on to the iron sheet that covered the brazier, rolled off that and lay on his back across the legs of the other runner, who had been crouched beside the brazier. In the bright light it was as if a whole pail of scarlet paint had been dashed across the man's face on the left and his chest. It glistened in the firelight—just like fresh paint, moving! (p. 307)

This is vivid writing and not easily forgotten. It is only possible when (as Ford would say) the novelist has prepared his effects, as we have seen him doing. But the technical problem raised by writing of this sort—with its hard cameo outlines—is a matter of continuity: how to get on, how to mediate between one scene and the next. The very sharpness of impression prevents a flow, especially since anything like ordinary chronological sequence is avoided by Ford. Life does not narrate; it impresses itself upon our minds and senses; and that is what Ford sought through his brand of impressionism.

Ford's solution of the problem is hinted at in his curious, and controversial, little book on Joseph Conrad. He warns against the novelist's reporting whole speeches—for example, by a long-winded suburbanite in his garden:

> If you gave all these long speeches one after the other you might be aware of a certain dullness when you reread that *compte rendu*. . . . But if you carefully broke up petunias, statuary, and flower-show motives and put them down in little shreds, one contrasting with the other, you would arrive at something much more coloured, animated, lifelike and interesting.[4]

The same principle, I believe, holds true for the large garden that is a battlefield: by laying down "in little shreds" such motives as blood, noise, mud, battle neurosis, relations between officers and men, thoughts of home, sexual excitement, interest in nature, Ford creates an effect that might be thought of as fugal. Or—to alter the metaphor—like seeds, these motives will show a strong inclination to grow and force their way from one scene into the next, as they do so, undergoing often strange metamorphoses. They weave the parts of the book together—and do much more besides.

The image of dead O Nine Morgan will illustrate the method, whose blood "glistened in the firelight—just like fresh paint, moving!" The suggestions called to mind by fresh paint—its stickiness in particular—are horrible enough, but the last word caps them: *moving*! It sticks in our minds and Tietjens' (as the blood sticks on his shoes). Tietjens suffers a series of recalls. Particularly interesting is the way that death and his wife's sex mania are drawn together in most of these, as though the motive were a rope with strands in two different colors. The first recall comes the same evening when, tucked up in

[4] Ford Madox Ford, *Joseph Conrad: A Personal Remembrance* (1924), p. 203.

bed in his fleabag, Tietjens is writing—jotting down as coolly and deliberately as he can, like a military estimate of the situation, the salient facts of his marital situation, hoping to find the answers to certain questions: *Has* his wife left him? Does that mean he will be free to live with Valentine Wannop? Should he? His thoughts are interrupted by the orderly, who is carrying on a doleful conversation with an officer in another part of the tent, concerning the evening's casualty. Tietjens hears the orderly say:

> "Poor—O Nine Morgan! . . ." and over the whitish sheet of paper on a level with his nose Tietjens perceived thin films of reddish purple to be wavering, then a glutinous surface of gummy scarlet pigment. Moving! (p. 355)

The second recall, coming two days later, is not of the blood directly but of a slowly moving brass door handle. The handle evokes a scene rather different from the replacement depot hut: a bedroom in an elegant hotel in the nearby town, where we find Tietjens with Sylvia, half-dressed, who has materialized in France with the same violence with which Poor—O Nine Morgan burst into the hut, made his succinct report and dropped dead. To create trouble Sylvia has left her bedroom door unlocked. An intoxicated M.P. colonel breaks in and is physically ejected by Tietjens, who as a consequence is placed under arrest and confined to his quarters. But General Campion, wishing the whole thing hushed up, comes the next morning to inspect Tietjens' unit and orders him to accompany the inspecting party on its rounds. (The general and Tietjens both know that this in effect releases him from arrest.) Also, and compassionately, the General sends in by his aid, Colonel Levin, a bottle of smelling salts, since Tietjens is understandably a bit shaky. But these do not have at all the bracing effect desired:

> Tietjens asked himself why the devil the sight of that smelling-salts container reminded him of the brass handle of the bedroom door moving almost imperceptibly . . . and incredibly. It was, of course, because Sylvia had on her illuminated dressing-table, reflected by the glass, just such another smooth, silver segment of tubing. . . . Was everything he saw going to remind him of the minute movement of that handle? (pp. 448–449)

The analogy between the two movements—the blood and the door handle—and the two scenes apparently does not occur to Tietjens, the bond being an unconscious one.

In the painful interview with the General that follows, Tietjens receives a movement order—to the front (to which he desperately doesn't want to go). He has, after all, been on his feet for two days and has suffered a series of shocks. He panics rather badly. It is mud that particularly upsets him, and with the news of his movement order comes another involuntary memory—of the trenches. Mud not only rhymes with blood, and is sticky like it, but it also sometimes moves—horribly.

In November. . . . A beginning of some November. . . . With a miracle of sunshine: not a cloud: the mud towering up shut you in intimately with a sky that ached for limpidity. . . . And the slime had moved . . . following a French bombardier who was strolling along eating nuts, disreputably, his shoulders rolling. . . . *Déserteurs*. . . . The moving slime was German deserters. . . . You could not see them: the leader of them—an officer!—had his glasses so thick with mud that you could not see the color of his eyes, and his half-dozen decorations were like the beginnings of swallows' nests, his beard like stalactites. . . . Of the other men you could only see the eyes—extraordinarily vivid: mostly blue like the sky! (pp. 486–487)

The final recall—coming late in the volume—is, appropriately, undisguisedly of O Nine Morgan, once again coming by way of Sylvia. Near the close of the interview the General, now adopting a fatherly or avuncular tone, asks the one question that for Tietjens is the most upsetting: "Why don't you divorce?"

Panic came over Tietjens. He knew it would be his last panic of the interview. No brain could stand more. Fragments of scenes of fighting, voices, names, went before his eyes and ears. Elaborate problems. . . . The whole map of the embattled world ran out in front of him—as large as a field. An embossed map in greenish *papier mâché*—a ten-acre field of embossed *papier mâché*: with the blood of O Nine Morgan blurring luminously over it. (pp. 492–493)

This motive of O Nine Morgan's blood is merely a single instance; in *No More Parades* and the tetralogy as a whole are dozens of others. What Ford said looking back at *The Good Soldier* applies also here: "I will permit myself to say that I was astounded at the work I must have put into the construction of the book, at the intricate tangle of references and cross-references."[5] And, in *Parade's End* at least, it is a tangle that *moves*—and not a tangle either but a fugue, as scene follows scene threaded on not one string but many.

2

The surprising thing for the hopeful reader of Ford is how little that moves and is moving is to be found in the twenty-odd other novels of his, books that seem often to have been written with tongue in cheek—what Ford called his "*pastiches,*" "*tours de force,*" and "pieces of rather precious writing."[6] Ford's first novel was published in 1892 and his last in 1936, yet except for about a decade, approximately 1914 to 1928, he is not a first-rate novelist. Even in such dismal failures as *Ring for Nancy* or *Vive Le Roy* many of the familiar Fordian techniques turn up—"the time-shift, the *progression d'effet,* the adaptation of rhythms to the pace of the action"[7]—and many of the themes. But actuality, inevitability, the unity of a growing thing—these we look for in vain. Why? The reason is partly to be found, I believe, in Ford's curious—and curiously dependent—relation to his subjects.

He was an occasional novelist as some men (Dryden comes to mind) were occasional poets, but unfortunately he needed for various reasons to go on writing whether there was an occasion or not. Indeed, his true occasion was single, unique—not even warfare, as with Hemingway, but a particular war, the "Great War." What came before was a preparation. Ford rose to the occasion splendidly and then for his last ten years subsided into the novelistic equivalent of anagrams or acrostics, the elaborate amusements of "an old man mad about writing." It was not that he was lacking in subjects for novels, but after *The Last Post* Ford could find none he could take quite seriously.

I have mentioned Dryden, but there is a better analogy in Wordsworth, who like Ford had the sensibility but too often seemed to lack the subject. " 'I want a subject.' Thus Wordsworth would, or could,

[5] Ford Madox Ford, *The Good Soldier: A Tale of Passion* (1951), p. xx. Subsequent page references will be to this edition.

[6] *Ibid.*, p. xviii.

[7] *It Was the Nightingale*, p. 6.

or should have begun his poem in fourteen books about himself." So Mark Van Doren begins an excellent essay on *The Prelude* in which he suggests that "Wordsworth created modern poetry when he decided that the man who writes is more important than the men and the things he writes about." Van Doren thinks "Wordsworth had special reasons for deciding this: he did not know men, and the fountain of things had dried up. The world was a barren place, producing no further mythologies. The poet stood alone, and without a lyre. If poetry was to live again, he must make it live from nothing. He must make the dry bones sound."[8]

Now Ford clearly did not believe the writer was more important than the men or the things he wrote about, and yet at far too tender an age—while still in his thirties—he brought out his first book of personal reminiscences and he went on bringing them out, volume after volume, to the end of his life. Some are excellent of their kind (an impressionist kind), but they end by usurping for him the place of genuine fictions altogether. It might be argued, too, that Ford was of course not a poet—a novelist rather, quite a different beast—but that, I think, would be wrong. Ford *was* a poet. It is not that his verse is of much account, though it has had its admirers. I have in mind rather the novels and in particular the thematic interweaving of the sort we have been examining: the images of movement, of blood and door handles, maps dissolving in red and florid colonels breaking into bedrooms. Here he is a poet. Though Ford had wanted, perhaps more than anything, to be a dispassionate observer of manners along the lines of Henry James, he became in fact something quite different.

We might remark it was not for not trying. Ford confessed that he had written early two *pastiches* in James's manner, and in *A Call* he nearly matched James in giving us the London of teas and wedding receptions, leisure and talk, but of a period slightly later than any rendered by James. But the texture of their writing is not the same. For one thing, though the impression of conversation often recurs, in Ford's novels very little is actually given; even that little is rather commonplace and, by Jamesian standards, without much subtlety.

[8] Mark Van Doren, "The Prelude," *The Noble Voice: A Study of Ten Great Poems* (New York: Henry Holt, 1946), p. 303.

In depicting their affairs both writers sought unity—all the unity they could get. (Ford believed the novel should be the rendering of "one embroilment, one set of embarrassments, one human coil, one psychological progression."[9]) But their ways of achieving unity were different.

James's method was dialectical. Mind is held against mind by the long conversations, disputes, debates—as those between Strether and Maria Gostrey in *The Ambassadors*—in which everything is known at any moment except the real point at issue. As Miss Gostrey herself says, to Strether, at the very end of the novel, " 'I never quite knew *where* you were. There were moments,' she explained, 'when you struck me as grandly cynical; there were others when you struck me as grandly vague'."[10] For us to have such books at all, the characters must possess extraordinary sensibilities and verbal gifts. And there for Ford was the rub. The Jamesian "interlocutor" may have been in the Victorian scene a justifiable exaggeration, but for a later day he was plain wrong. Ford knew that few of his contemporaries were conspicuously articulate. In his book on Conrad he wrote: "If you listen to two Englishmen communicating by means of words, for you can hardly call it conversing, you will find that their speeches are little more than this: A. says, 'What sort of a fellow is . . . *you* know!' B. replies, 'Oh, he's a sort of a . . .' and A. exclaims, 'Ah, I always thought so'."[11] Consequently long conversations in the manner of James were out.

Instead of the extraordinary moral sensibility, Ford was drawn to the most ordinary, the mind of the "average man" (who had for him something of the fascination of a fabulous monster). He writes in *Women and Men*: "We all have very strongly within us the belief that there is such a thing. The belief is as strong as that in the immortality of our souls. And we think, when we are not thinking about it, that we know a large number of quite average men and women. We should laugh loudly if . . . told that we could not put our finger immediately upon a perfectly average man or . . . woman. And yet, the moment you

[9] Ford Madox Ford, *Return to Yesterday* (1932), p. 203.

[10] Henry James, *The Ambassadors* (New York: Harper & Brothers, 1948), pp. 413–414.

[11] *Joseph Conrad*, p. 143.

come to try to do it, you will find that it is absolutely impossible."[12] "You meet," he explains elsewhere, "an English gentleman at your golf club. He is beefy, full of health, the moral of the boy from an English Public School of the finest type. You discover, gradually, that he is hopelessly neurasthenic, dishonest in matters of small change, but unexpectedly self-sacrificing, a dreadful liar but a most painfully careful student of lepidoptera and, finally, from the public prints, a bigamist who was once, under another name, hammered on the Stock Exchange. . . . Still, there he is, the beefy, full-fed fellow, moral of an English Public School product."[13]

To see men in this double fashion is to begin to recognize their absurdity. Ford's characters, though they may at first appear as beefy, full-fed fellows, do not remain so in our eyes for long. It is in their sundry falls—or breakdowns—that he subjects them to experiences that are less horrible than macabre—and absurd. Particularly in the earlier novels (as with Dudley Leicester in *A Call*) Ford seems to find it hard to take their predicaments seriously; his writing before long begins to burlesque both the poor puppets and itself. He seems to be saying: "This is absurd, but *life* can't be as absurd as that!" If I read Ford correctly, it took nothing less than the approach of the First World War to shock him into a recognition of how truly absurd the human predicament was.

The war, then, helped to define Ford's subject for him. It is here that he comes to resemble Wordsworth. Van Doren has suggested that Wordsworth, despite his difficulties in finding an adequate subject for the great poem that he never came to write, had in fact a hidden subject of whose existence perhaps even he was only partly aware—and further that it underlay *The Prelude*, the *Intimations* ode, and most of the *Lyrical Ballads*. This hidden subject was the French Revolution, about which Wordsworth had, as we know, painfully mixed feelings. He could not accept its disorder, violence, and bloodshed, yet at the start he had been almost a sans-culotte. For years it was to remain a challenge to his not yet fully set complacency. Van Doren thinks Wordsworth could ease his tensions only by staging a small

[12] Ford Madox Ford, *Women and Men* (1923), p. 47.
[13] *Joseph Conrad*, pp. 136–137.

revolution of his own, undertaking to substitute for the Revolution's "public program of reconstruction by reason a private program of resurrection by feeling" (p. 240). Each lyric was made to contribute to that program. As long as Wordsworth's doubts about the Revolution lasted he was thus a troubled man but a happy poet; it was only when they gradually disappeared, after Napoleon and, later, the restoration of the Bourbons, that his stimulus came to an end and inspiration ran dry. His subject had slipped away, and it was only then that a daffodil no longer spoke to him.

For Ford the equivalent of Wordsworth's Revolution was of course the War—or, as he was wont to call it, Armageddon. It was for him the end of the world, *his* world. We know from reading other, mostly younger, men how disturbing that first world war was, even to some who saw only a little of it. Ford was in the army four years. At the start he was a man already in his forties, sedentary, somewhat neurotic, fat—hardly a military type. Besides, personal reasons must have made this war particularly shocking and painful for him. Ford was half German: his father, Franz Hueffer, had come from Westphalia; he had himself passed part of his youth visiting family in what he called "High Germany." Though Ford had a lifelong detestation for Prussia, he had warm feelings for that other, smaller Germany of high gables and light rain—and for its poetry, with which he would have liked to identify his own:

> I would give almost anything to have written almost any modern German lyric or some of the ballads of my friend Levin Schücking. These fellows you know. They sit at their high windows in German lodgings; they lean out; it is raining steadily. Opposite them is a shop where herring salad, onions and oranges are sold. A woman with a red petticoat and a black-and-grey-check shawl goes into the shop and buys three onions, four oranges and half a kilo of herring salad. And there is a poem! Hang it all! There is a poem.[14]

Obviously it was not pleasant for Ford to find himself fighting "these fellows."

But the War fascinated and distressed Ford in other ways. Perhaps more to the point, and certainly more in line with the view I have been

[14] Ford Madox Hueffer, *Collected Poems* (1914), p. 12.

trying to develop, was its sudden emergence as the outward and visible sign of an inward and spiritual disgrace: the social, or cultural, disarray that such novels as *A Call* or *Mr. Fleight* were already, if fumblingly, trying to express. It became in fact his perfect subject. What Ford as a man was to lose in the War was considerable: before it was over he was gassed and shell-shocked, and he was destined to return to an England where he felt a stranger and which seems to have held no place for him. But as a novelist it was under that sign that he would conquer. His best work was written between the approach of war and the end of the twenties; it records the debacle, his own and his society's. Even when the War is not directly present (as in most of *The Marsden Case*), it informs his vision. It is the hidden subject. In *Parade's End* it takes the center of the stage. There Ford treats of a falling asunder, a cultural dismemberment, followed by the barest hint of a regrouping. But art is happier than life, and these extraordinary novels, never harrowing though containing their share of horrors, comprise a late-won and lasting synthesis.

3

In *Parade's End* much comes together—aspects of Ford's thought and art that previously were scattered piecemeal, "probably lost, as isolated chapters in unachieved and too-quickly-issued novels."[15] Yet *Parade's End* is not the result of a slow, sustained development and could hardly have been predicted by Ford's early readers. In this respect the pattern of his creative life is a queer one. The development of many—probably most—novelists and poets may be compared to British constitutional history, where precedent slowly broadens down to precedent. Henry James would be such a novelist: there is the apprentice work followed by the first successes, then the long middle period, the late flowering, and the final lessening efforts; but the end is implicit in the beginning, though it is an extension and an enrichment—and there is substantial accomplishment at many points along the way. Ford is not like that. His career is as improbable as that of

[15] See Ezra Pound, "Ford Madox (Hueffer) Ford; Obit." *Furioso*, I, 3 (Spring, 1940), 3.

a man destined to become a great chef who began early in childhood making fudge, learned in adolescence to boil eggs, mastered salads at eighteen, peppermint candy at twenty, cream sauce at twenty-six—and then suddenly, and amazingly, at forty-one cooked his first full dinner, and it was a masterpiece! (If my simile has a facetious appearance, it is one I think Ford would have accepted.) His first published novel, written in his teens and called *The Shifting of the Fire*, was the story of an octogenarian English gentleman named Kasker-Ryves, who wishing to destroy his young wife hit upon the original device of simply wearing her out by the activity of their social life during the London season—but instead he wears himself out and dies grotesquely. This early attempt—which Joseph Conrad called "delightfully young"—was followed by as queer an assortment of unlikely fictional situations as one can readily imagine: an invasion from the Fourth Dimension, a London visitation by the god Apollo, witchcraft on the high seas, the therapeutic use of giants at a German sanatorium, though here and there is interspersed a bit of more solid fare such as *The Benefactor* or *A Call* or *An English Girl.* Then suddenly, and as if from nowhere, appeared *The Good Soldier* and the Tietjens tetralogy.

Probably I exaggerate. We cannot say with confidence that any of it is irrelevant to the final accomplishment, since Ford learned his craft and his (by no means sullen) art at these unlikely endeavors. But it does remain unpromising to study him soberly period by period, as James or Conrad can be studied with profit, or Flaubert or Thomas Mann. He constitutes a special problem. One possible approach to Ford's development is suggested by Richard A. Cassell and worked out with thoroughness in his *Ford Madox Ford: A Study of His Novels.* "No one seems to have questioned," Mr. Cassell remarks, "that *The Good Soldier* and *Parade's End* are his fictional masterpieces. It is probable that they did not just happen or spring spontaneously from his imagination. It would seem . . . that his early novels somehow prepared him for his major work."[16] The question is of

[16] Richard A. Cassell, *Ford Madox Ford: A Study of His Novels* (1961), pp. ix–x.

course how? One way of answering that question is to go for the themes and techniques, and that is Mr. Cassell's way. It is a matter of bringing them into line. Most of Ford's critical writing has remained out of print and is hard to come by. Cassell quotes liberally from such books as *The English Novel, The March of Literature*, and *The Critical Attitude*. He in fact does what it seems doubtful Ford ever did, he assembles an inclusive and consistent theory of fiction by drawing a little here and a little there, and extends this method to Ford's political, or social, attitudes, the "themes" of the novels. He then shows that both techniques and themes are operative in the first novels as well as the last, though somehow more vigorously operative in *The Good Soldier* and *Parade's End* (which appear after all to be the best of the lot). Such an orderly approach has a good deal to recommend it; it would be carping to remark that it is perhaps too orderly. Yet I am not persuaded that consistency was ever Ford's most striking characteristic.

Be that as it may, my own concerns are different. They are restricted to one phase—the major phase—of Ford's career: his novels that center on the war. If Ford did not have a vision of his world (not many writers since Dante have had a vision of their world), he did have, especially at the end, a number of *views* about the world. Yet vision remains the right word—though a vision not of the world as it might have appeared during most of his sixty-odd years but as it was at a moment of crisis, a particular convulsion. Ford recorded in a half dozen brilliant books the debacle of an already debased society. However, *debacle* denotes "a breaking up of ice in a river," "a violent rush of waters"; it is a freeing as well as a catastrophe. Both aspects are there and both must be taken into account. In *Parade's End* in particular these crosscurrents of feeling are given form and are preserved, not just in occasional set speeches but in the whole intricate patterning of the narrative.

In the chapters that follow I propose to consider Ford Madox Ford's war novels with reference to various elements, some formal, some perceptual, some rather strange, that have come together under pressure. What are these? Most are found in the sequence from *No More Parades* which we have been examining, our diamond of pattern. There they are fused, joined without seam, as they tend to be throughout the Tietjens books. It is a good deal easier, however, to isolate them for inspection in the earlier attempts, *The Marsden Case* and its milder counterpart *No Enemy*, where many of the elements of Ford's vision join without ever coming into exact harmony or focus. These earlier books are also of much interest in their own right.

ii. LANDSCAPES AND INTERIORS

The by-streets were amazingly quiet; closed houses, shuttered shops, mostly unhurt; not a soul was in the blazing sunlight; not a cloud was in the sky; only, in the dust of the road three cats were motionlessly intent on love.

—*No Enemy*

Ford's war is not quite the war of any other writer and his soldiers are not quite like any other soldiers; they seem older, sadder, quieter, though occasionally they are given to outbreaks of sudden gaiety, kick footballs across no man's land, and toss hats into enemy trenches. For the most part, though, they are thoughtful and responsible souls, both terribly homesick and yet somehow strangely at home as they lounge in jerry-built armchairs constructed from bully-beef cases or wait their turns for a bath in a great, steaming, abandoned mill, some chatting gravely, some reading Henry James. Ford's is not a young man's war, certainly not Ernest Hemingway's war. For most novelists the key fact of war and not-war (one hesitates to say peace) is their separation. The soldier, in action and out, is hardly the same man. When Hemingway's Lieutenant Henry is busy retreating from Caporetto, he is busy retreating from Caporetto, winging deserters, dodging Austrians, and so on; when he is safe in Milan eating midnight sandwiches with Catherine Barkley, he is eating midnight sandwiches —and never the twain shall meet. Not so with Ford's soldiers. Each is, as Ford put it, "*homo duplex*: a poor fellow whose body is tied in one place but whose mind and personality brood eternally over another distant locality."[1]

[1] Ford Madox Ford, *It Was the Nightingale* (1933), p. 217.

Or at least that is the impression Ford gives at his most characteristic and best, in *Parade's End* and intermittently in *The Marsden Case* and *No Enemy*—his comparative failure in the earlier books being the measure of his eventual success. Though sifting war through peace and peace through war seems in the Tietjens series as naturally sustained as breathing, it is rather the slowly acquired result of craft and art. Or (to shift the metaphor) if peace and war are the two halves of Ford's world, in the earlier books they do not quite fit: he can see both vividly enough but has not found the novelistic way—not yet—of seeing them quite steadily and whole.

The Marsden Case was the first published though not the first written; it is more conventionally a novel than its companion, is ultimately less interesting, more uneven, and is consequently probably best considered first. It imposes upon the experience of war the pattern of death and rebirth; that is, its protagonist in the course of the story, and during wartime, is deprived of his name, is hanged, cut down; he then stands up, assumes a new name and a new persona and at the end is as glorious as a lord—which he has in fact become. When we first see George Heimann, however, a few weeks before the outbreak of war, he is caught between the notorious old world dying and a new world as yet powerless to be born. The opening scene takes place in the backroom of a dishonest publisher's office "walled-in completely with books that all wore their paper wrappers."[2] It is a gloomy and depressing place.

> In such a place books are at their most sinister and their most forlorn. They await sales, and are I suppose more new than they will be if ever they reach the booksellers' shelves; but they appear wearisomely old, with the oldness of a last week's daily paper. Upon them there will be always a film of dust, and they fit too rigidly into the white deal shelves. A limbo of books! A place where the Unborn float pallidly in dimnesses! (p. 1)

The protagonist is not, as we might suppose, an author; and perhaps that is a mistake after such an opening. But he is first encountered there by the narrator Jessop, who *is* an author—young George Heimann having come to beard the publisher in his den. *The Marsden Case* opens on the dying prewar world; it makes the summer of 1914

[2] Ford Madox Ford, *The Marsden Case* (1923), p. 1.

as tangible as London fog. "I don't know," Jessop writes, "if you remember the season of 1914, in London and the world over. It comes back to me as a period of outcries, smashings, the noises of broken glass falling to the ground and physical violences. An accursed year!" (p. 13)

Before turning our thoughts to George Heimann let us briefly consider what appears to be his genesis, his way of materializing (as it were) out of that period and out of a particular scene, for he has at least one recognizable prototype. It is fitting that the focal scene of Part One of *The Marsden Case* should be an underground night club, an unventilated purlieu recalling the infernal atmosphere of the publisher's inner sanctum. Its original has been described in a recent letter by Ezra Pound in his characteristic telegraphese:

> The Cave of the calf was started by Frieda.
> "And are you any connection of THE Strindberg?"
> responsus:
> Yesss, I ahm vun of his Wives.
> and to me: "I needt money. I haff therefore dagen upp brosstiDuchun, in tdiss bardicular form."[3]

Ford has taken over Madame (dark-brown accent and all). He seems also to have drawn on another underground dive, the scene of the disagreeable Imagist dinner given by Amy Lowell at which he first took notice of the young sculptor Henri Gaudier-Brzeska, who was later killed in the war. Like Heimann, Gaudier stood out as a radiant being against a murky background. Ford has described the occasion as follows:

> It was an "affair" . . . financed by a disagreeably obese Neutral whom I much disliked. That would be in late July, 1914. The Neutral was much concerned to be out of a country and a city which appeared to be in danger. Some one else—several some ones—were intensely anxious, each of them, to get money out of the very fat, very monied, disagreeably intelligent being. . . .
>
> There were also speeches—and one could not help knowing that the speeches were directed at the Neutral's breeches pockets. . . .

[3] See Eustace Mullins, *This Difficult Individual, Ezra Pound* (New York: 1961), p. 98.

> Then Gaudier rose. It was suddenly like a silence that intervened during a distressing and ceaseless noise. I don't know that I had ever noticed him before except as one amongst a crowd of dirtyish, bearded, slouch-hatted individuals, like conspirators; but, there, he seemed as if he stood amidst sunlight; as if indeed he floated in a ray of sunlight, like the dove in Early Italian pictures. In a life during which I have known thousands of people; thousands and thousands of people; during which I have grown sick and tired of "people" so that I prefer the society of cabbages, goats, and the flowers of the marrow plant; I have never otherwise known what it was to witness an appearance which symbolized so completely—aloofness. It was like the appearance of Apollo at a creditors' meeting. It was supernatural.[4]

George Heimann is similarly attired (Inverness cape, beard, slouch-hat) and on Mr. Jessop makes a similar strong impression.

It is just three weeks before the outbreak of war. Heimann is in an uncomfortable position. He is the translator of a dull German poem, *The Titanic: An Epic*, written by his good friend one Professor Curtius. He knows the poem is what it is. Nevertheless, he must see the publisher do the poet justice, at least financially. George Heimann is only twenty-two. Though he is not from the Midi (as Gaudier was), George's mother was French and came from Arles; she has been dead for some time and George and his younger sister Mary Elizabeth have been brought up on the Continent by an "uncle" whom they must think of as Mr. Heimann but who is in reality, they discover, the self-exiled Earl Marsden. The sister is the cause of most of George's present troubles. It is she who has pressured him into the scene with Podd; she has also been insisting that he force the Earl to acknowledge his paternity and their legitimacy. This George has refused to do, with the result that their position in England remains ambiguous. During the nasty scene in the publisher's office Podd calls the young man a bastard; yet later he is the one who brings action for libel, an action that (England being what it is at the moment) enmeshes George Heimann in an atrocious tangle of misunderstandings. By developing this tangle Ford recaptures something of the hatefulness of the summer of 1914 and of the early war years.

Unfortunately the plot is exceedingly complex, melodramatic,

[4] Ford Madox Ford, *No Enemy* (1929), pp. 205–207.

whimsical, sentimental—and often it is plain tiresome. At times *The Marsden Case* reads like a cruel parody of the author of *The Good Soldier* and *Parade's End.* Fortunately the plot does not really get under way until Part Two; the interim is Ford's. Part One is a very detailed and often intriguing rendering (134 pages) of a single day, beginning in Podd's office and ending late that night. The crucial night-club scene is made to suggest the moment when all London, on the eve of war, goes underground. This feeling of fevered strangeness was foreshadowed in Podd's anteroom by the strange names of his assistants when he called them to his side for protection or to serve as witnesses: "Absalom! Oneday! Byles! Miss Ketch!" (p. 11) It began on the moment shortly before, when Podd and Jessop, entering the anteroom, first discovered George's presence:

> A man in silhouette like a chimpanzee was crouched in a bent-wood chair over a deal table. Mr. Podd, intent on finding some book and browsing at once along the shelves, did not notice him at all. I suppose he took him for his chief assistant, who must really have gone to lunch. Mr. Podd muttered:
>
> "*The Palace of Peace!* Where's *The Palace of Peace?* It ought to be here!"
>
> Suddenly he switched on an electric light in a shadeless bulb, and the place grew brilliantly sordid. (p. 3)

This is followed by high words and Podd's accusation of bastardy. But soon "the rapidities of the London season of 1914" sweep narrator and reader on past luncheon to a Ladies Club where the narrator is to speak in opposition to "some such motion as: 'That the Irish are a Race of Poets' " (p. 18). Jessop is by this time doubly upset: "The manuscript of my shadow play—which was to be produced that night! —was, so far as I knew, still lost. It had been stolen by a consumptive Russian tenor. That sounds improbable, but, as far as I knew, it is true" (p. 40). With all this on his mind, he yet manages to debate with someone who seems very much like W. B. Yeats. At last the afternoon is behind and Jessop, George Heimann, and a lovely young actress, Clarice Honeywill, proceed "down the yawning, black stairs of the Night Club."

"We were at the bottom of the stairs, and the fantastic vista of that home of orgies opened before us, a dim cellar in which, in what daylight filtered down, all shapes were grey. At a considerable distance, over some tables, Madame was moving desultorily. Though it was mid-July she was wrapped up in an immense fur coat" (p. 88). This is evidently Hades, the abode of shadows (in the present instance the setting for a shadow play). Jessop partakes of food in this underworld; thereafter, by the time-honored principles of magic, he will be its prisoner.

> Madame was wavering towards us, a rather shapeless black shadow, coming deviously, between the little tables, her face gradually swimming up, chalk-white. In the whiter reflections of that sheet [prepared as a screen for the shadow play] she held, just protruding from a furred sleeve, an enormous peach. She placed that in my left hand and then, withdrawing into her sleeve-hole, protruded a small white cylinder of paper that dropped on to the marble table-top. She looked slowly round at the sheet and drifted away.
>
> The young people seized on that manuscript and ran off.
>
> A waiter in his shirt sleeves was at my elbow. He bore on a silver tray four admirable—four wonderful—sandwiches that contained immense prawns, a long-necked green bottle of Moselle and a tall, greenish drinking glass.
>
> I ate ravenously. The young man who had designed the silhouettes for the shadow-play passed swiftly before the screen, a cardboard box beneath his cape, himself a silhouette. In costume he was an exact replica of George Heimann, only he was not quite so tall. That was uniform, really, for certain dashing young men. Well, they had uniforms enough a very little later. (pp. 89–90)

It is all very real, very unreal—shadowy. Yet after the promising start in Part One the novelist falters. Ford hurries and fumbles as he spins his elaborate intrigue. In the remainder of the book too many developments are crowded into too narrow a space, a failure that tends to make everything seem a bit ridiculous, as in a speeded-up movie from the incunabula of the films.

There is a mad chase to Germany to bring back the Earl—unsuccessful, since the Earl took his life on the morning of August 4, hanging himself from a low beech tree. George is imprisoned by the Germans, later released at the instigation of the author of *The Titanic: An Epic.* He manages to get back to England, enters the Guards, serves for a few weeks and is discharged at the instigation of his trouble-making sister. His serious trouble begins then. In the guards he was sheltered and happy, but once out he is miserable. George is hounded by a malicious press and an increasingly hysterical populace. In London his German landlady is killed and her house burned. When he moves to the country to live with Mary Elizabeth (who is now the widow of Jessop's brother), he finds it even more trying. Ford traces George Heimann's decline to a decisive moment under a beech tree that Jessop learns of only indirectly when another character (one of Ford's obtuse stock Americans) remarks, "George is all right. I have kept my eye on him. He wrote some letters. Now he has gone up there with a rope" (p. 319).

This attempted suicide is the main peripety. George is discovered before it is too late, and thereafter his situation improves as he comes more and more under the protection of his good angel, the young actress with the appropriate name of Clarice Honeywill (she is clear-minded, strong-willed, but sweet). He had made a slight miscalculation: the beech tree was too low and, Clarice arriving in the nick of time, he was cut down. Hereafter she does what is needed to counteract Mary Elizabeth and when the War is over and George's legitimacy has been established, she marries her Lord Marsden and they live happily forever after.

Part Two of this fable is devoted to the War years, with a brief final chapter set some time after the Armistice. The narrator all this while has been in the service, most of the time in France; by the conclusion of hostilities he—like Tietjens and like Ford—has suffered a bad mental breakdown. Part Two contains the memorable passage:

> I used to think that, once out there, we should be surrounded by a magic and invisible tent that would keep from us all temporal cares. But we are not so surrounded, and it is not like that. The one nail does not knock out the other. There is that never ceasing waiting about; and the cold; and the long depressions. Now and then there is terrible noise—wearing, lasting for days. And some pain. All that is bearable. But what is desolating, what is beyond everything hateful, is that, round your transparent tent, the old evils, the old heartbreaks and the old cruelties are unceasingly at work. (p. 305)

But Jessop only tells us this, he does not show it. The emphasis in *The*

Marsden Case is all on the old evils; the invisible tent we are asked to take on faith—with the consequence that even the old evils are rather hard to believe in. Perhaps if Ford had continued on the scale and in the tempo of the opening sequence and had developed his characters, the result might have been something to put beside the Tietjens trilogy. As it is, after a good start *The Marsden Case* is abortive.

2

Ford's narrator Jessop insists that he is writing no war novel, although *The Marsden Case* is a novel in which the war plays a part; in contrast *No Enemy* is about war directly, although it may not be a novel. Then again it may; it all depends. In 1929 Ford wrote to his agent Eric Pinker about *No Enemy*: "It was written as to one chapter, in the front line, and as to the rest just after peace was declared. I thought at the time that it was too personal to publish at once and determined to keep it for ten years which have just elapsed. It won't appear in New York till November."[5] Later, after its publication in this country, Ford wrote to Hugh Walpole:

> Pinker declares that no English publisher that he has approached will touch it which rather astonishes me for it has had quite a remarkable reception in the United States where they say it is a monument of prose which it probably isn't but when you consider that it is the war-reminiscences of the only British novelist of anything like, say, my age who actually took part in hostilities as an infantry officer it seems singular that no one should want to print it as a document.[6]

It is neither a monument of prose nor merely a curious document but is, I submit, after all a novel (and a most readable one) if we judge the matter not by whether a story is being told or whether—supposing there is a story—it is true, but by the form of the book and the quality of its writing. *No Enemy* opens shortly after the end of the war upon a small house in the country not far from the sea, a house made famous by lines in Ezra Pound's "Hugh Selwyn Mauberley":

[5] See David Dow Harvey, *Ford Madox Ford, 1873–1939: A Bibliography of Works and Criticism* (1962), p. 74.

[6] *Ibid.*, p. 74.

Beneath the sagging roof
The stylist has taken shelter,
Unpaid, uncelebrated,
At last from the world's welter.

Nature receives him;
With a placid and uneducated mistress
He exercises his talents
And the soil meets his distress.

The haven from sophistications and contentions
Leaks through its thatch;
He offers succulent cooking;
The door has a creaking latch.

The protagonist is an English poet with a French name, Hippolyte Gringoire, "Gallophile, Veteran, Gardener and, above all, Economist, if not above all Poet" (p. 10). He lives with one Madame Sélysette (who seems to be neither placid nor uneducated); she is "meridional," of the "haute bourgoisie." The third principal character is called simply Compy: he is a compiler, a sort of Boswell to Gringoire's Johnson, who visits from time to time to take down his reminiscences which differ from most in being "the war-reminiscences of a contemplative and sensitive soul." "One can only console one's self that when it comes to war-reminiscences the contemplative and sensitive soul has been little represented. So, for the matter of that, has the poetic but economical chef" (p. 12).

However, these are more than war reminiscences, as the compiler makes clear:

This book, then, is the story of Gringoire just after . . . Armageddon. For it struck the writer that you hear of the men that went, and you hear of what they did when they were There. But you never hear how It left them. You hear how things were destroyed, but seldom of the painful processes of Reconstruction. (p. 9)

So there are to be two main themes or motifs: war reminiscences and the peaceful but strenuous present; the story of a soldier and the story of a farmer-poet. Of course, Gringoire is pretty much Ford, at least in his military role: the war poems, supposedly by him, quoted here and there are Ford's "Clair de Lune," "The Old Houses of

Flanders," and "Footsloggers"; we are told that he is the former owner of *The English Review*, that his grandfather was born in Calais, and so on. On the other hand the tale of Gringoire's reconstruction, the scenes with Compy and Sélysette are fiction—apparently—along with the "great, half-finished epic" which Gringoire is writing and about which we hear from time to time. Compy even is in some ways nearer Ford than Gringoire, since he is a prose writer and looks down on Gringoire's "poet's prose." The result is a curious brew: the war scenes are real, or at least realistic, the peace scenes fictional, suggesting a fairy tale. The little cottage is under a cliff of rock "like a gingerbread house from a Grimm's fairy tale"; a nearby nightingale, wandering into the garden because it has young to feed, is imagined as "a princess turned housekeeper"; while at other times the fairy tale appropriately has about it a touch of terror, as when Gringoire wonders how the wiggly lines of his handwritten manuscripts can ever be "the barbed wire fence that shall keep the wolf from the door of the cottage? Why, he could push the poor, tindery old walls down with his snout!" (p. 223)

"I have tried then to write a novel drawing my material from my own literary age. You have here two adventures of a once *jeune, homme pauvre*—a poor man who was once young. In rendering them, I have employed every wile known to me as a novelist—the time-shift, the *progression d'effet,* the adaptation of rhythms to the pace of the action."[7] Ford is speaking here of a later book of reminiscences whose subject in part overlaps the subject of *No Enemy,* but all that he says is truer I think of the earlier and better "novel." Above all, *No Enemy* is a memory book:

> A French critic having said that I was one of Proust's closest imitators I was in a position to say . . . that I had never read a word of Proust. And having then worked myself in my mind into the strategic strongpoint that I desired to occupy I at once bought a copy of "A Côté de Chez Swann." I read it and "A la Recherche du Temps Perdu," in one weekend at Guermantes and I found in Proust's work all the supernatural hypnosis that his most devoted followers obtain from it. But I do not think I have imitated him since.[8]

[7] *It Was the Nightingale*, p. 6.
[8] *Ibid.*, pp. 292–293.

To be is to be remembered, he might have said. This is the War as seen in perspective, the perspective of peace, glimpsed as if over the shoulder from the "gingerbread cottage"; war re-collected from its fragments by a curiously tricky and sensitive mind. Setting aside the question of influence, there is an affinity between the two authors and particularly in *No Enemy*, which more than anything else written by Ford suggests Proust—but a more benign, less erotic, decidedly more masculine and more military Proust.

At the start Gringoire wonders whether his experience of landscape during the War was that of many people. It was as though color had gone out of the land, as though everything were covered by a gray mist coincident with the countryside's becoming merely a congeries of landmarks to be quickly noted and acted on by the practical will. So in crossing a field "it was Headquarters one wanted, not the storing of the mind with observed aspects" (p. 24). During the whole War he *observed* only four—or perhaps it was five—landscapes. Now at odd moments these come back to him unsolicited and apparently will stay with him always, memory having belonged to them from their first observation.

They were, those intermissions of the spirit, exactly like gazing through rifts in a mist. Do you know what it is to be on a Welsh mountain side when a heavy mist comes on? Nothing remains. You are there by yourself. . . . And the only preoccupation you have with the solid, invisible world is the boulders over which you stumble and the tufts of herbage that you try to recognize as your path. Then suddenly the mist is riven perpendicularly, and for a moment you see a pallid, flat plain stretching to infinity beneath your feet and running palely to a sea horizon on a level with your eyes. There will be pale churches, pale fields, and on a ghostly channel the wraiths of scattered islands. Then it will be all gone. (p. 24)

The first such intermission of the spirit was a moment early in the War when Gringoire, temporarily at rest, sat in Kensington Gardens watching some Guardsmen doing unfamiliar drill. His eyes and mind wandered briefly; then suddenly

there were great motionless trees, heavy in their summer foliage, blue-gray, beneath a very high sky; there was the long, quiet part of the palace; the red brick, glowing in the sun, the shadows of the windows very precise and blue. And Gringoire thought that old, stiff marionettes, rather homely courtiers and royalties, might step out of the tall windows onto the lawns. (p. 25)

The impression lasted only for an instant and then was gone.

There was a similar moment later when on driving into a small country railroad station he learned of the death of Lord Kitchener—a shock but not a cause for personal grief. The whole War seemed to fall away leaving Gringoire sitting on a wooden bench with legs thrust out: "And so the veil lifted for a second. The flat lands of Essex were there, stretching out; flat fields; undistinguished beneath a dull sky" (p. 34). Then the War closed in again.

The other intermissions are more interesting since they occurred near the front. One was a glimpse of balloons, Gringoire's first, over the shoulder of a great down—a skyscape really and not a landscape.

> They appeared to be globes, because there was a fresh wind blowing straight from them and they turned end on. So, but slowly and incessantly heaving, did the immense one close at hand; a spider's network of cordage went with its movements. Tiny and incredibly pretty, like films of gold dust floating in blue water and like peach blossom leaves—yes, incredibly pretty in the sunlight—airplanes were there. (p. 59)

Of the remaining two the first was even less a landscape but a moment of exaltation transfiguring Gringoire and everything around him. He had been dozing in a hillside dugout with a sheet-iron roof, across a corner of which the wheel of a passing field gun rolled, tilting it and then letting it fall with a crash. A bad moment. Now long afterwards, in England, as he listens to the distant Portsmouth naval guns firing target practice against a background of birdsong, he remembers the scene that followed the bad moment in the dugout. As he had come striding down the hill feeling understandably glad to be alive, an "innumerable company" of swallows, rising from the ground,

> flew round him, waist high, just brushing the thistledown. "They were so near," Gringoire said, "that they brushed my hands, and they extended so far that I could see nothing else. . . . It is one of the . . . things of the war that I really see, for it was like walking, buoyantly, in the pellucid sunlight, waist-high through a sea of unsurpassed and unsurpassable azure. I felt as if I were a Greek god. It was like a miracle" (p. 44).

The last is more conventionally a landscape, a great view from the top of Mt. Vedaigne:

The red roofs of a village that he knew to be Wytschaete were brilliant and quiet in the sun—but, on the brown line beneath that ridge the little white balls went on coming into existence—one every half second. One to the right at the extreme end of the line; one on the extreme left; one in the middle; one between the extreme left and the center. Beautiful work. Have you ever seen a village cobbler nailing a sole? It goes so quickly that you hardly see the hammer. But a small brass nail is there—and another and another—a line of brass nails on the smooth leather. Well, they went like that, along the brown line—the little white balls! Beautiful! Beautiful work. (pp. 83–84)

It raises a question that may also be raised by the other exhibits: is vision of this sort to be construed as sensitivity or insensitivity? Has Gringoire forgotten what the little white balls really are? No, I think he remembers. His rendering of aspects is not to be confused with the notorious confession (made, I believe, by one of Mussolini's sons) of the pleasure to be derived from the flowerlike pattern that sometimes comes into being when an antipersonnel bomb is dropped among tightly massed men. Ford or Gringoire—whichever it is—is not trafficking here in sadistic titillations but is recording the peaceful dimension of violence. As a foot soldier he is aware there are others.

3

Landscapes are necessarily somewhat indifferent to man, and so long as an observer's eye is fixed on the landscape he must be indifferent too. It is to houses, not fields, that we go for the pathos of the human condition. "Possibly the idea of country—just country—postulates the idea of human companionship—but that is not the same thing as humanity" (p. 124). The landscape was there before man and it will be there after man is gone; but houses are man's creation, the extension of his being; they both contain the human and are contained by it. Particularly after dark they have a human look. We say, "That house appears to be winking; that other is gnashing green teeth!" (pp. 167–168) When they die it is almost sadder than when men die because—so Ford thinks—houses have no immortal souls. Once gone, they are completely gone. Nothing is more forlorn than the shell of a house, no roof, not much in the way of walls, no window panes—yet lace curtains still blowing in and out of the windows and pictures still hanging on what walls are left. All this must be remembered: such interiors and others less violently smashed serve as the necessary corrective to the serene indifference of the great view.

No Enemy is arranged accordingly, the first part "Four Landscapes," the second "Certain Interiors." In contrast to the landscapes, which are sunlit, tranquil, and remote, these interiors—as interiors in war must be—are usually dark and often painful. Indoors, Gringoire never feels like a Greek god. At one extreme is the interior of a French ministry, all marble and filigree, with Swiss guards in antique uniforms standing about—the scene of an embarrassing interview. It calls to mind another disagreeable scene, at night, taking place upon a balcony at the Comédie Française in the presence of covertly hostile and rather patronizing French officers. They are talking, reproachfully, of their dead. This in turn causes Gringoire to recall a very different interior, a steamy army bathhouse in Albert where he had once sat reading *What Maisie Knew* while listening intermittently to the life story of the attendant, a talkative Canadian in his sixties, a tired man who was later killed.

Darkest and best are various interiors in Pont de Nieppe, a semi-evacuated town in the combat zone. Ford catches the exact feel of such a place. One rainy night, in his capacity as billeting officer, Gringoire seeks out the town mayor, whom he finds at last improbably in a dentist's waiting room (his own, since he is also the town dentist) containing "aspidistras, black walnut furniture, and innumerable copies of the illustrated paper called *Excelsior* on the lace table-cover" (p. 239). During his search down various rain-swept streets Gringoire gets soaked—to the wrists, something he detests—and the whole sequence ends with him seated at last in a firelit kitchen, stripped to the waist, while a Belgian woman who is the temporary occupant of the house sews placidly, although every few minutes the pots jump on the stove as shells land in a church eighty yards away. This is the one bright indoor scene in the book.

Throughout *No Enemy* Ford withholds the worst horrors. His interiors are muted rather than monstrous. He does not dwell on burning houses or dying men, though both are implied. Instead he depicts the routine discomforts, the cold, the bad smells, the hunger. His examples of heroism are also played down. A Jewish woman about to be evacuated stands in her rag-and-bone shop quietly folding quantities of black petticoats while shells drop all around outside, until one finally lands on the second floor, sending miscellaneous junk tumbling down the stairs. She goes on folding. She has her counterpart in a splendid old line officer, rather drunk, who is on hand the first time Gringoire is under artillery fire and who refuses to budge from his tent—even after a shell hits the canteen next door and sends a can of sardines sailing into Gringoire's lap. And there are others.

As with the shadow play in *The Marsden Case*, so here in these interiors with their quiet and brave occupants there is an odd unreality —the shadow of the absurd, which is not an unreality that (like leprechauns) one can easily shrug off. The dentist's untouched waiting room in otherwise badly smashed Nieppe was prepared for by these remarks about detraining near the front:

> It was rather like a dream—not at all a bad dream—but, anyhow, a numbness. Or no: really it was more like being in the hands of doctors, on the way to an operation. . . .
>
> In the same way you may remember the anteroom of your dentist. There is a big table in the center of the room; on the table some writing materials—and old periodicals. . . . The street, then, is real: and the operating room will soon feel as real, even while one is waiting in the outer room. But the anteroom itself is a dream-landscape. (pp. 51–52)

This dreaminess lends a "distancing" to Ford's interiors which permits them to interlock with his visionary landscapes: they are war seen more intimately, with more concern for the combatants and the civilians, their homes, hopes, goods and chattels, but still war seen with a certain detachment. "We were all," as Hemingway's convalescent soldier remarked, "a little detached."

4

After the beautiful restrained depiction of the insides and outsides of the life of those who fight, it is disappointing to have to acknowledge that Ford in the peace part of this little *War and Peace* fails; the clean line is lost in whimsy and sentiment. As a tale of combat *and* reconstruction *No Enemy* does not hold together. It is evidently by detachment, unreality, and the shadow of dream that Ford hopes to make his war scenes of a similar density to his scenes of peace stylized as they already are by the fairy-tale motifs. If that is his intention in *No Enemy*, however, he does not succeed. The wartime landscapes and interiors do go together remarkably well, but his war and peace finally do not. He does not see the two steadily; perhaps he does not even try to. The laconic Gringoire of the trenches and the windy, fluttery, always very self-centered moralist and amateur chef of the Gingerbread Cottage do not seem the same man—a failure that, as I suggested earlier, is a measure of Ford's success with his characters in *Parade's End*.

Indeed the war and peace portions of *No Enemy* might almost have been written by different men; they read like an only moderately successful collaboration. Revealing in this connection is a remark that is let drop near the end of the book by Gringoire, who is struggling to translate a letter that he wrote earlier in French: "He couldn't, as he said, translate his own French prose because his own French was near his heart and his English much less. You might say that his passions were for English countrysides and for French prose and here the two met to his confusion" (p. 285). In *No Enemy* the sentimentalized English countryside with its nightingales and flowerbeds and Haensels and Gretels (imported from Germany) and the dispassionate accurate prose that made a constatation of the war in France meet to Ford's confusion. Yet these two very different sides of Ford's sensibility, and his art, can meet more happily—and do in *Parade's End*—to make what they never quite make here: a single strange vision that partakes about equally of Gustave Flaubert and fairyland.

iii. SOME BORROWINGS FROM FRANCE

He added—and how sincerely and with what passion—putting one hand on his chest and just bowing, that he loved and had loved France as he had never loved a woman!
—*Return to Yesterday*

It seems appropriate that Ford Madox Ford's maternal grandfather was born in France, in Calais, and appropriate that he was a painter. In Ford's novels the effects are very often painterly—and nearly always French. In "getting in" an interior—and especially in *Parade's End*—he will characteristically give the source and quality of light, perhaps no more than the glimmer from a "bucket pierced with holes, filled with incandescent coke" (p. 221) or it may be the brilliance of a "bar of light that the sunlight threw in at . . . [the] open door" (p. 444). Ford's eye had been trained early in the studio of his grandfather, and it is appropriate also that his first book as an adult was a critical biography written immediately after Madox Brown's death, when Ford himself was scarcely twenty. Vision for him was to remain a matter of *vision*, of how things looked. This later became a bond with Joseph Conrad of whom Ford said: "We had the same aims and we had all the time the same aims."[1] He was referring to their consuming interest in the visible.

Their visual aims—and the techniques that went with them—by 1913 Ford was calling "impressionism,"[2] a term taken of course from the history of painting. Applied to writing, it is a slippery and not

[1] Ford Madox Ford, *Joseph Conrad* (1924), p. 179.

[2] See Ford Madox Hueffer, "Impressionism—Some Speculations," *Poetry*, II (August, 1913), 177–187; also "On Impressionism," *Poetry and Drama*, I, 6 (June, 1914), 167–175.

altogether fortunate term. Ford's impressionism is clearly not Walter Pater's, for example, or even quite Conrad's, probably because in Ford's case there was the corrective of music. His father, Francis Hueffer, was a music critic of some distinction. According to Goldring, "In such a musical household . . . it was natural that he should spend much of his time at the piano and begin to make attempts at musical composition."[3] We are told that Ford even thought of making a career of music. In the end, his development as a writer probably owed about as much to the one art as to the other: painting stressed the importance of the image; music served as a reminder of time.

However, the strongest immediate influence was literary and came from France. In *The March of Literature* Ford remarked: "Nearly all Mediterranean writers and critics acknowledge that if you want to write you should have some—nay, as much as possible—knowledge of the technique of your art. Nearly all Nordic writers and critics contemn the idea."[4] Today that has the sound of an exaggeration. We tend to forget that in Ford's youth in England the novel was not yet regarded as an art form. As its then greatest practitioner and theorist put it:

> I suspect . . . that one would not be far wrong in saying that in addition to the people to whom it has never occurred that a novel ought to be artistic, there are a great many others who, if this principle were urged upon them, would be filled with an indefinable mistrust. They would find it difficult to explain their repugnance, but it would operate strongly to put them on their guard. "Art," in our Protestant communities, where so many things have got so strangely twisted about, is supposed in certain circles to have some vague injurious effect upon those who make it an important consideration, who let it weigh in the balance.[5]

When Henry James made this statement in England eighty years ago he was very much a lone voice. It would have been quite different in France—was different. Ford thought James to be French in derivation: "Diderot begot, as you might say, Chateaubriand and even

[3] Douglas Goldring, *Trained for Genius: The Life and Writings of Ford Madox Ford* (1949), p. 41.

[4] Ford Madox Ford, *The March of Literature* (1938), p. 531.

[5] Henry James, "The Art of Fiction," *Partial Portraits* (New York: Macmillan, 1888), pp. 379–380.

Stendhal; and Stendhal and Chateaubriand between them had for children Flaubert, Maupassant, the Goncourts, Gautier, and the very air of the very circle in which Turgenieff and the young James went about together."[6] It would not be wrong to see Ford himself as deriving from James and from Conrad, who was more French even than James. But he also learned something from the French novelists directly.

When, near the turn of the century, Ford and Joseph Conrad, behind Conrad's mare Nancy traveled the country roads near the Pent farm, the older writer would ask from time to time such a question as, "Well, Ford, *mon vieux*, how would you render that field of wheat?" —and they would have a go at it. Their method, Ford explains, was bilingual. First they would hit on the *mot juste*, or *phrase juste*, in French—usually without too much difficulty—and then they would try with considerable furrowing of brows to English it.

> *Champs de blés que les vents faibles sillonnaient.* . . . Cornfields. . . . No, not cornfields, because that, to Americans, signifies maize. . . . Wheat fields. . . . Fields of wheat that the weak . . . feeble . . . light . . . what sort of winds, breezes, airs. . . . Fields of wheat that small winds ruffled into cat's-paws. . . . That is, of course, too literary.[7]

Always the French phrases came first, as apparently they did when Conrad was writing. Ford concedes that Conrad "could naturally write, 'Will you have a cup of tea?' or 'He is dead,' without first expressing himself to himself in French. But when he wrote a set of phrases like . . . 'the pulsating stream of light,' or 'the deceitful flow from the heart of an impenetrable darkness,' he was translating directly from the French in his mind."[8] It was through this exercise (or word game), and through collaborating with Conrad on *The Inheritors* and *Romance*, that Ford learned to write English prose—or learned some of the difficulties of writing English prose. Indeed, in collaborating with Conrad he had most of the benefits of translating from a foreign tongue.

[6] Ford Madox Hueffer, *Henry James: A Critical Study* (1913), p. 55.

[7] *Joseph Conrad*, pp. 26–27.

[8] *Ibid.*, pp. 168–169.

What would these be? At the very least a certain linguistic perspective. Where the foreign tongue is a Romance language there is the added benefit of drill in that second language within the English language composed of the long Latin words that have never quite been naturalized—"pulsating," "impenetrable," and, as Conrad uses it, perhaps even "deceitful": resonant words traditionally serviceable in heightening a style ("multitudinous," "incarnadine"). But for Ford I think it was the former benefit that mattered most, since in his eyes English was probably already if anything too rich. He complained:

> No English word is a word; . . . all English words are instruments for exciting blurred emotions. 'Oaken' in French means 'made of oak wood'—nothing more. 'Oaken' in English connotes innumerable moral attributes: it will connote stolidity, resolution, honesty, blond features, relative unbreakableness, absolute unbendableness—also, made of oak . . . The consequence is that no English word has clean edges: a reader is always, for a fraction of a second, uncertain as to which meaning of the word the writer intends.[9]

It is by his translating that the bilingual writer sharpens the edges of his words. The best way I know to suggest what this discipline meant to Ford is to quote his extended passage of analysis of the opening sentence of Flaubert's "Un Coeur Simple." This first appeared in Ford's book of wartime propaganda, *Between St. Dennis and St. George*. "Un Coeur Simple" begins: "Pendant un demi-siècle, les bourgeoises de Pont-l'Evêque envièrent à Mme. Aubain sa servante Félicité." Ford's comment follows.

> This simple sentence is the beginning of the story which, at this moment [the war year 1915], is of most significance to the world. It means that for fifty years the middle-class housewives of Pont-l'Evêque envied Mme. Aubain her servant Félicité. Nevertheless, exactly and rightly to translate that simple sentence is a task of almost unheard-of difficulty. Let us consider for a moment these verbal exactitudes. Let us take the words "*Pendant un demi-siècle.*" If we say "During half a century," the words have not a quite English sound. If we say "For fifty years," the period is too exact in appearance. It would give the suggestion that Mme. Aubain was about to celebrate a golden jubilee. And the opening words of a story

[9] *Ibid.*, p. 229.

are of immense importance because they strike a note in the reader's mind, so that if we start the reader anticipating the celebration of a golden jubilee, and if no such celebration take place, the reader's mind will be a little confused. In the French the sentence suggests no event of any kind, not so much as the shadow of an event. The clear, cold sentence, with its cadence just sufficiently long to leave the reader wishing for the next syllables, dictatorially limits the mind to the consideration, firstly, of Mme. Aubain, and then, by the careful reservation of the servant's name to the last words, indicates with absolute precision that the main interest of the story will be the servant Félicité. The use of the word *bourgeoises* indicates that Pont-l'Evêque is a town, or a large village, of sufficient importance to contain several families in fairly comfortable circumstances. The note thus exactly struck in the reader's mind amounts to this: that the story will concern itself with an affair lasting fifty years, that the affair will not contain any memorable events, and that it will centre round the life of a faithful servant—for Félicité was for fifty years in the service of her mistress, and the other housewives of the place envied Mme. Aubain.

We must therefore not commence our rendering by saying "For fifty years." On the other hand, "During half a century" is not quite right. I do not know why it is not quite right—I fancy that the word "during" rather implies sequences of similar or dissimilar but not continuous actions spread over a given period. I think we should be using correct English—correct idiomatic English—if we said "During the next two centuries the Danes made repeated attempts to break the power of the Heptarchy"; but I think we should have to say "For the last twenty-five years"—or, if we wanted to be more literary—"For the last quarter of a century Admiral von Tirpitz was, or has been, unceasingly engaged in the long effort to raise a High Seas Fleet for the German Empire."

Thus, in the case of Félicité we might say that for half a century the housewives, etc. On the other hand, "For half a century," is too literary a phrase to satisfy an absolutely delicate ear. Personally, if I were writing the story on these lines I should begin with an exact statement of the number of years, softening off the exactness with the qualificative "more than." "For more than thirty-seven years," I should say, and I think I should arrive at about the sense of Flaubert's phrase.[10]

Ford then works over the word *bourgeoises*, rejecting *housewives* (" 'housewife' is a dangerous word because, in its proper pronuncia-

[10] Ford Madox Hueffer, *Between St. Dennis and St. George: A Sketch of Three Civilisations* (1915), pp. 199–201.

tion of 'hussif,' it sounds too like 'hussy' to go near the word 'envied' ") and changes "envied Mme. Aubain her servant" to "envied Mme. Aubain because of her servant." He explains:

After the word "envied" I have inserted the words "because of," so as still further to get away from the implication of mortal sin. For it seems to me that if I say: "I envy So-and-So his position," that might mean that I was attempting to get him out of his job, and to obtain it for myself; whereas, if I say that I envy him because of his position, it would at the most imply that I should like to have a similar one.

He concludes: "The reader will say, 'What is the use of all this fuss about the exact incidence of a few commonplace words?' I can only answer that the exact use of words seems to me to be the most important thing in the world."[11]

The resulting style is in some danger of being finicking. In his own early writing it sometimes is. Recognizing the danger, Ford warned the would-be writer that the *mot* should not be allowed to become too *juste*:

A style interests when it carries the reader along; it is then a good style. A style ceases to interest when by reason of disjointed sentences, over-used words, monotonous or jog-trot cadences, it fatigues the reader's mind. *Too* startling words, however apt, *too* just images, *too* great displays of cleverness are apt in the long run to be as fatiguing as the most over-used words or the most jog-trot cadences. That a face resembles a Dutch clock has been too often said; to say that it resembles a ham is inexact and conveys nothing; to say that it has the mournfulness of an old, squashed-in meat tin, cast away on a waste building lot, would be smart—but too much of that sort of thing would become a nuisance. . . .

We [Ford and Conrad] used to say that a passage of good style began with a fresh, unusual word, and continued with fresh, unusual words to the end; there was nothing more to it.[12]

Take the following passage, praised by Ford in his introduction to the Modern Library edition of Ernest Hemingway's *A Farewell to Arms*:

[11] *Ibid.*, pp. 202–203.
[12] *Joseph Conrad*, pp. 206–208.

I was in under the canvas with guns. They smelled cleanly of oil and grease. I lay and listened to the rain on the canvas and the clicking of the car over the rails. There was a little light came through and I lay and looked at the guns.

It is disarmingly simple. Ford comments upon the word "cleanly":

The guns smelled cleanly of oil and grease. Oil and grease are not usually associated in the mind with a clean smell. Yet at the minutest reflection you realise that the oil and grease on the clean metal of big guns are not dirt. So the adverb is just. You have had a moment of surprise and then your knowledge is added to.

And he finishes by saying: "The word 'author' means 'someone who adds to your consciousness' " (pp. xvi–xvii).

That is what Ford does superbly in his own war writing.

So much for words. Speaking of himself and his famous collaborator, Ford once said: "Our attributes were no doubt different . . . [I] probably knew more about words, but Conrad had certainly an infinitely greater hold over the architectonics of the novel, over the way a story should be built up so that its interest progresses and grows up to the last word."[13] This was true for the years of their collaboration, at least; what Conrad already knew about design Ford was still trying to learn. At the start they had agreed "that a poem was not that which was written in verse but that, either prose or verse, that had constructive beauty. We agreed that . . . what the novel needed was the New Form."[14]

What was the New Form? Or would there be a New Form for each new novel? Probably not, although the New Form remained for some time elusive. At times it seemed to Ford to lie in a fancied resemblance to musical development—as with the sonata—a suggestion that in later years he attributed (oddly) to H. G. Wells:

One day he said to me, "What do you say, Fordie, to giving a novel the form of a sonata?"

I jumped a little. I had never imagined Mr. Wells as taking interest either in novel forms or in music.

[13] *Ibid.*, p. 179. [14] *Ibid.*, p. 30.

"You know," he went on, "first subject: Hero. Second subject: Heroine. Because you must never introduce your hero and heroine in the first chapter. It's uneconomical. . . . And then Working Out and Recapitulation."[15]

Wells incidentally denied the story. It was nevertheless an original idea and perfectly feasible. *A Man Could Stand Up*, for example, follows sonata form. In Part One the first subject is introduced and then developed: the heroine Valentine Wannop, surrounded by schoolgirls, in London on the morning of Armistice Day. In Part Two the second subject is introduced: the hero Christopher Tietjens, surrounded by Tommies, in the trenches some months earlier. In Part Three, the late afternoon of Armistice Day, the two are brought together and there is a working-out as earlier motifs are restated, played off, varied, repeated, and finally resolved.

The sonata form is appropriate here, where Ford is concerned with a hero and heroine long-separated and then united; but it would not be appropriate for many situations. So far as I know, there is nothing quite like it in Conrad's novels or in others by Ford, for sonata form is only incidentally Ford's New Form. Besides, the parallel is not very exact. In a late book Ford claimed that novels possess "a form, even as sonnets and sonatas possess forms";[16] but unfortunately that is not so. In the one case the form is given, in the other it must be found. Though there are many forms that might be found for the novel, the New Form of Ford and Conrad derived ultimately from the behavior of language itself—from words used as an impressionist would use them.

"The main and perhaps most passionate tenet of impressionism," Ford wrote, "was the suppression of the author from the pages of his books. He must not comment; he must not narrate; he must present his impressions of his imaginary affairs as if he had been present at them."[17] For illustration Ford proposes that we take the following (imaginary) sentence from *Vanity Fair*:

Disgusting as we may find it, on crossing to the window our heroine—whom the reader must acknowledge to be indeed a gallant little person—

[15] Ford Madox Ford, *Portraits from Life* (1937), p. 111.

[16] Ford Madox Ford, *Return to Yesterday* (1932) p. 202.

[17] *The March of Literature*, pp. 840–841.

perceived Captain Crawley and the Marquis of Steyne engaged in a drunken boxing bout.

That would not be impressionism. Suppose, however, the author had written:

In the street the empurpled leg-of-mutton fist of a scarlet heavy dragoon impinged on the gleaming false teeth of a reeling baldheaded senior. Becky screamed as a torrent of dark purple burst from the marquis' lips to dribble down his lavender silk waistcoat.[18]

That would be impressionism, since the action is not stated but is suggested. Ford remarks that it would not be very good impressionism, being rhythmically jog-trot (on the order of "The quick sly fox jumped over the lazy brown dog") and "verbally overvivid." But it is a good self-parody.

Impressionism of this sort, easily taught and easily learned, has become the period style for the mid-twentieth century—the style of the *Saturday Evening Post.* We forget that in Conrad's day it was fresh and new. But to apply the same principle to the design of larger units is another matter, for their New Form is still not generally understood. After half a century it is still new.

Ford believed the great innovator here was Stendhal, especially in the war chapters of *La Chartreuse de Parme*, where impressionism, rather than logic or narrative sequence, governs the form. These chapters

must be the most dispassioned of all constatations of the purposeless and imbecile helplessness of war and of troops in action. His projections of Fabrice's ride over the field of Waterloo in the staff of Marshall Ney—on to which that stripling has got by pretending to be the lover of the wife of one of Ney's cavalry captains—is a nightmare of aimlessness. Compared to it the most depressed pages of Tolstoi's *War and Peace* read like inadequate witticisms.[19]

Stendhal composed by juxtaposing; he assembled incongruous incidents much as an impressionist sentence assembles incongruous par-

[18] *Ibid.*, p. 841.
[19] *Ibid.*, p. 780.

ticulars. In *The March of Literature* Ford sets down the principle with unusual care:

> The juxtaposition of the composed renderings of two or more unexaggerated actions or situations may be used to establish, like the juxtaposition of vital word to vital word, a sort of frictional current of electric life that will extraordinarily galvanize the work of art in which the device is employed. That has the appearance of being a rather hard aesthetic nut to crack. Let us put it more concretely by citing the algebraic truth that $(a + b)^2$ equals not merely $a^2 + b^2$, but a^2 plus an apparently unearned increment called 2ab plus the expected b^2.[20]

He leaves it to us to supply examples; one thinks of the handling of the agricultural exhibit in *Madame Bovary* or of the tournament in Allen Tate's *The Fathers*. Or let us suppose a scene where one safecracker is discovered quietly picking his teeth while his buddy is picking a lock. The reader may smile (Kenneth Burke's "perspective by incongruity"); but the juxtaposition also tends to make both actions seem more real. The electric current of actuality begins to flow, and this unexpected sense of life is the "apparently unearned increment."

Restraint is necesary; the juxtapositions must not appear too incongruous. The desired effect is rather of "ordinariness set against ordinariness in a slightly different plane."[21] So, though Stendhal's battlefield of Waterloo is a much queerer place than most in the pages of fiction, it is also more ordinary. There is among novelists an honored convention that battlefields are strictly off-limits to civilians, though the battlefields of this world in fact are seldom without a few farmers, herders, or washerwomen going about their normal business, drawing water from wells, stealing, or simply looking for souvenirs. Stendhal writes as though he had never heard of this convention. At Fabrice's side there is a motherly, middle-aged woman, semicivilian, a *cantinière* or seller of grog to the soldiers. She combines two distinct kinds of ordinariness in her own commonplace person. As saleslady with an eye to the profit motive, she is eminently a representative of

[20] *Ibid.*, p. 804.
[21] *Ibid.*, p. 807.

that other world behind the lines; yet she is a hardened veteran as well. It is the *cantinière* who witnesses Fabrice's initiation; she is the godmother at his baptism of fire. The scene that follows is a good example of Stendhal's method, as ordinariness is set against ordinariness in a different plane—the ordinariness of peace against the ordinariness of war.

It turns on Fabrice's shaking hands, the most ordinary of acts, particularly for a Latin. Encountering the dead is also an ordinary act for hardened campaigners like the *cantinière*—but not, of, course, for Fabrice. Here is Stendhal putting the elements together, making his juxtapositions:

> Fabrice n'avait pas fait cinq cents pas que sa rosse s'arrêta tout court: c'était un cadavre, posé en travers du sentier, qui faisait horreur au cheval et au cavalier.
>
> La figure de Fabrice, trés-pâle naturellement, prit une teinte verte fort prononcée; la cantinière, après avoir regardé le mort, dit, comme se parlant à elle-même: Ça n'est pas de notre division. Puis levant les yeux sur notre héros, elle éclata de rire.
>
> —Ha! ha! mon petit! s'ècrià-t-elle, en voilà du nanan! Fabrice restait glacè. Ce qui le frappait surtout, c'était la saleté des pieds de ce cadavre qui déjà était dépouillé de ses souliers, et auquel on n'avait laissé qu'un mauvais pantalon tout souillé de sang.
>
> —Approche, lui dit la cantinière, descends de cheval; il faut que tu t'y accoutumes. Tiens, s'écria-t-elle, il en a eu par la tête.
>
> Une balle, entrée à côté du nez, était sortie par la tempe opposée, et défigurait ce cadavre d'une façon hideuse; il était resté avec un oeil ouvert.
>
> —Descends donc de cheval, petit, dit la cantinière, et donne-lui une poignée de main pour voir s'il te la rendra.
>
> Sans hésiter, quoique près de rendre l'âme de dégoût, Fabrice se jeta à bas de cheval et prit la main du cadavre qu'il secoua ferme; puis il resta comme anéanti: il sentait qu'il n'avait pas la force de remonter à cheval. Ce qui lui faisait horreur surtout, c'était cet oeil ouvert.[22]

This quiet passage makes some of Flaubert's more famous ironies seem almost obvious, as in the contrapuntal scene of the Agricultural Exhibit in *Madame Bovary*, where Rodolphe dazzles Emma with talk about "elective affinities" in a room overlooking the square while a

[22] Stendhal, *La Chartreuse de Parme* (Paris: C. Levy, 1887), p. 37.

speech about the need to improve manures keeps the farmers spellbound down below. But the method in both is juxtaposition. Stendhal's turn of mind, however, is less deliberate, and the result is more fluid and surprising. It anticipates Proust; for example, the horrible scene where Françoise is discovered brushing vigorously the long hair of the grandmother whose head, now that she is immobilized—and for Françoise dehumanized—by a stroke, bobs helplessly in the servant's hands. Stendhal's passage anticipates also some of Ford's own queerer effects.

"We used to say . . . that a subject must be seized by the throat until the last drop of dramatic possibility was squeezed out of it. . . . From this the novel got its unity. No doubt it might have its caesura—or even several; but these must be brought about by temperamental pauses, markings of time when the treatment called for them."[23] It is this last, casual sentence that is revealing. It points to something that is only latent in the writing of Flaubert and Stendhal: time regarded as a major aspect of form in the novel. It was here that the English writers were to make a contribution of their own.

Time can enter a story in a number of different, if related, ways. There is first the time required for reading it, which varies from reader to reader but is roughly predictable. There is the time covered by the story—was it an hour, a month, a year? This is a matter of watches and calendars, but there is also subjective time of various sorts—or may be. To one of the participants it may have seemed an eternity. There may also be past time remembered (as with a drowning man) and future time anticipated (as with a patient in the dentist's waiting room). When the novelist begins to concern himself with the shifting interrelations between these, some intriguing possibilities occur. By rearranging his ingredients, by putting in a little more of this and less of that, he may hope to thicken or thin the narrative line at will and so, eventually, compose his patterns in time.

Control of these elements depends on the discovery—or rediscovery, for the time-shift is as old as Homer—that where time in the world can never reverse, in fiction it can. Before Conrad, novels usu-

[23] *Return to Yesterday*, p. 203.

ally went straight ahead. Now and then there might be a flashback near the beginning of a long novel, but it seems to have occurred to no one to try to make continual shifts in time enter the very texture of the narrative (not even in *Tristram Shandy*, an apparent exception, for in Sterne's queer book there *is* no narrative). Conrad was in these matters the great innovator. Probably his most radical departure from chronological sequence is to be found in *Heart of Darkness*, where the story begins in the present on the crusing yawl *Nellie*, turns back to Marlow's early visit to Belgium, moves ahead to the Congo taking us up the river with great leaps in time, more flashbacks, and occasional returns to the yawl *Nellie*. Conrad never handled his method more successfully than here (*Chance* seems a comparative failure), and not until Ford's *The Good Soldier* was there any further significant advance in this mode of composition. In that novel Ford was to go Conrad one better.

Of the two friends Conrad was in nearly every respect the less sedentary, both as writer and man. Each of his stories is at some level an adventure story, a prolonged chase through a forest of symbols. Ford's characters on the contrary are usually "pinned down": by their wives, their worries, their bad debts, by paralysis, mutism, or even enemy gunfire. Like the two prostrate giants in his story "Riesenberg," they are the constitutionally immobilized; but while their bodies lie dormant and their wills are often frustrated, they lead the active inner lives of all worriers, waiters, and reminiscers. Their thoughts move backwards and forwards in the slow spiral of time. *The Good Soldier* is written accordingly: spun in time, it is a tissue of analogies and composed juxtapositions.

Apparently it was this aspect of Ford's writing that John Rodker had in mind when he made about it his often repeated observation. A young admirer having said one day of *The Good Soldier*, "By Jove, this is the finest novel in the English language," Rodker (with "properly tempered admiration") replied: "Ah yes. It is, but you have left out a word. It is the finest French novel in the English language!"[24] Rodker's is a handsome if somewhat ambiguous compliment. This earlier novel of Ford's is a fine one. It incorporates the various tech-

[24] Ford Madox Ford, *The Good Soldier* (1951), p. xx.

niques we have been considering; yet it concerns us perhaps even more in our present inquiry as a reference point for understanding the later, larger, more various *Parade's End.* As the story of a British officer it also attaches (more than tangentially) to the present subject.

2

Despite the promise of its title *The Good Soldier* is not usually thought of as a war book, its hero Edward Ashburnham being the most peaceful soldier imaginable: a retired British Army captain who never saw a shot fired in anger except in border raids in India, and who died of a self-inflicted penknife wound several months before the Germans crossed the Belgian frontier on August 4, 1914. *The Good Soldier* is the story of two couples, one English, one American, who for nine years met annually at Bad Nauheim for the cure—Ashburnham was said to suffer from "a heart"—and who formed an intimacy that seemed to be singularly peaceful. "Upon my word," the narrator Dowell remarks, "our intimacy was like a minuet, simply because on every possible occasion and in every possible circumstance we knew where to go, where to sit, which table we unanimously should choose; and we could rise and go, all four together, without a signal from any one of us, always to the music of the Kur orchestra, always in the temperate sunshine, or, if it rained, in discreet shelters" (p. 6). Nothing could be more remote, one might think, than this gentle and refined leisure from the world of bomb shelters, dugouts, barbed wire, mud, and mustard gas. And yet a distinguished contemporary poet who knew Ford has suggested otherwise:

> Ah Ford!
> Was it war, the sport of kings, that your *Good Soldier,*
> the best French novel in the language, taught
> those Georgian Whig magnificoes at Oxford,
> at Oxford decimated on the Somme?[25]

These lines by Robert Lowell are arresting, though their intent is perhaps not entirely clear: they raise the question of the relation between

[25] Robert Lowell, "Ford Madox Ford," *Life Studies* (New York, Farrar, Strauss and Cudahy, 1959), p. 49.

the fragile minuet and the noisier chords which so soon were to drown it out.

Ford tells us that on his fortieth birthday, December 17, 1913, he set to work on a novel that was to contain, as he put it, "*all* that I knew about writing." It was intended (for reasons that we need not go into here) to be his last book, his farewell to literature, but it was also to be his first, and only, novel—"novel" in an intensive sense, since Ford held lofty views about what a novel should be. Afterwards, he called the result his "great auk's egg," explaining that the great auk lays one egg and then bursts.[26] Though Ford had wanted to call this novel *The Saddest Story* his publisher objected, feeling in the war year 1915 that readers would prefer something more cheery. Ford seems to have been evasive and was slow to suggest an alternative title. Besides, though overage and corpulent, he was by that time "engaged in other pursuits." He tells how one day while on active duty he received from John Lane a wire appealing for a new title and replied ("in hasty irony") *The Good Soldier*. Six months later, to his horror, the book appeared under that title.

Why Ford should have felt horror is not easy to say, since *The Good Soldier* is a good title, certainly an improvement on *The Saddest Story*. But apparently he did; yet when it was reprinted in the following decade he thought it was already too late to make a change. He remarks in his Dedicatory Letter that if he had had a chance during the War he would have changed the title promptly then, since there had been only two occasions when anyone showed the least signs of having heard of his novel. (No doubt he exaggerates.) On one of the two times Ford's regimental adjutant just back from leave was showing a long face, which he explained was the result of having become engaged on one day and of having read *The Good Soldier* on the next. On the other occasion Ford was being examined in drill on the Guards' Square at Chelsea before "a half-dozen elderly gentlemen with red hatbands" and out of sheer nervousness got his men "hopelessly boxed." One of the reviewing officers walked close behind his back and said distinctly in his ear, "Did you say 'The *Good* Soldier'?"

[26] See Douglas Goldring, *Trained for Genius* (1949), pp. 173–181. Ford's own account of the genesis of this novel may be found in the Dedicatory Letter to *The Good Soldier* (1951) and in *Return to Yesterday* (1932), pp. 399–401.

So in this respect at least *The Good Soldier* was a war novel: it was published, perhaps partly written, during the War, and given its title during the War; its first readers were wartime readers; and the reviewing staff officer (the red hatband) perceived an identity between Captain Ashburnham and Captain Hueffer.[27] But the military title and the wartime circumstances of the book's publication are what may be thought of as extrinsic connections. Probably more germane is an important bit of internal evidence, the strange matter of the recurring date, to understand which it will be necessary to have in mind the main outlines of the plot.

The Good Soldier offers for our examination what its narrator Dowell calls a "little four-square coterie" (p. 5). According to *The American College Dictionary*, *foursquare* in its adjectival usage is the equivalent of "square," "firm," "steady," "frank," "blunt," and as an adverb means "without equivocation"—in fact, just the qualities that this coterie most lacked. It comprises a credulous and faithful husband (John Dowell) who is married to a faithless wife (Florence), and a faithless—or at least decidedly unfaithful—husband (Edward Ashburnham) who is married to a faithful but cynical wife (Leonora). What we have then is more than a triangle, and Ford showed great skill as a geometer of the heart. The two faithless and two faithful members suggest many intriguing analogies and differences, especially in the case of Edward and Florence, whom Ford brings together as lovers.

We are asked to believe that Edward's infidelities stemmed from his innocence of heart and were also partly in reaction to the misguided economies and austerities imposed by his cold, devoted wife. Edward began early on his divagations by kissing a mournful servant girl on a local train. It was done impulsively, mostly to cheer her up; but Edward found to his astonishment that he liked the sensation. (The servant girl evidently did not, since she pulled the emergency stop.) From this unpromising beginning he went on to various sentimental affairs with other, usually mournful, women. Florence Dowell's infidelities, on the contrary, were the result of no such innocence. Be-

[27] In the years 1914–1918 Ford was still Ford Madox Hueffer. His change of name did not come till later (June, 1919).

fore and during her marriage she was the mistress of a young man named Jimmy (significantly, his last name is never mentioned). The next man to enter her life had been Dowell; but Dowell was to be no more than a peg for her settled ambitions, which included living permanently in Europe and excluded intimacies with him. Immediately after their wedding, while on a rough Atlantic crossing, Florence feigned heart trouble, with the general aim of keeping Dowell off and of keeping him from suspecting her infidelities with Jimmy. Then, after Jimmy, there came Edward Ashburnham.

The Dowells and the Ashburnhams met at Nauheim. For nine years little happened outwardly; then there was a change. The denouement coincided with Edward's falling in love once more, and for the last time—with his own ward, a mournful, intelligent, and strange girl named Nancy Rufford. Discovering this, Florence Dowell, out of jealousy and despair (and perhaps vanity?), took poison and died; she had sensed Ashburnham's new love almost before he had. When Edward at last recognized what was happening, he did all in his power to hold off and for once he successfully resisted temptation. Though discredited by his wife in the eyes of the girl, Edward refused to be balked in his firm resolve to send Nancy back to her father in India. In return all that he asked was that she love him always. That is asking a lot. His entire sentimental being depended on it. This hope was shattered when Nancy out of mixed motives (part resentment at being sent away, part disillusionment, part native cruelty, and perhaps also part mistaken girlish sportsmanship) sent from Brindisi a cable with the laconic message, "Having rattling good time." Such unfeeling disregard for the tragedy he lived by proved too much for Edward, who quietly reached in his pocket for his fatal penknife. Nancy's cable was of course only apparently unfeeling. Upon receiving the news of Edward's death, she suffered a complete collapse, and at the novel's end we find her being cared for by Dowell, who has bought Edward's old home, Branshaw Teleragh, and has settled down to no future at all. And there the author takes leave of them.

The early reviewers—at least on this side of the Atlantic—were righteously indignant. "Realism and consistency are the sole virtues of the story," wrote the *Boston Evening Transcript*. "The portrayal of marital infidelity is dangerous enough even when delicately handled, and for the written page to linger upon the indecencies of intrigue—details, to be expected from the reeking tongue of the alley-gossip—there is no excuse whatever. For all the author's clever manipulation of words, he has given his story nothing to compensate for its artistic feebleness or to clear its distorted, sex-morbid atmosphere."[28] Today's judgment is of course rather different. For, though reduced to its essential plot *The Good Soldier* is melodrama of a vintage mellowness, complete with the savor of multiple adultery, madness, incestuous desires, two suicides, an escape from a second-floor window, the caning of an old Negro retainer, and so on, unfolded as Ford unfolds it the story does not seem much like melodrama but is as queerly insistent as life itself.

Things keep happening to (or through) Florence Dowell, eerily, on August 4 of various years: 1874, 1899, 1900, 1901, 1904, 1913. Florence was born on the fourth of August, set out to go around the world with her aged uncle on the fourth of August, became the mistress of a young man named Jimmy on the fourth of August, married poor John Dowell on the fourth of August, and reached a clandestine understanding with Edward Ashburnham on the fourth of August. Then, nine years later, she took her life on the fourth of August.

But why? What is the meaning of these compound coincidences that are something more than absurd?

First let me say what I think it is not. Coincidence pushed to such lengths is too dreamlike to function as irony. If one is somewhat accident-prone (to take a comparable instance), it is *not* ironical that during a single vacation he breaks a toe in the shower, dislocates his shoulder playing ball, and sits down in poison ivy while enjoying a picnic. It is simply the way things are, in a pattern that is unchangeable. Ford's coincidences are perhaps best seen as structural, as recurrences that serve to underline *The Good Soldier*'s massive stasis—for of all the novels[29] that come to mind it is the one that least moves ahead. Its technique depends throughout on the radical employment of time-shifts. The best brief description of what Ford is doing is perhaps the following sentence taken from Lawrence Durrell's *Justine*

[28] *Boston Evening Transcript*, Wednesday, March 17, 1915, p. 24.

[29] Close runners would be *Ulysses, Absalom, Absalom, The Alexandria Quartet,* and Conrad's *Chance.*

(1957); the Irish novelist Pursewarden is meditating on the "n-dimensional" novel: "The narrative momentum forward is counter-sprung by references backwards in time, giving the impression of a book which is not travelling from *a* to *b* but standing above time and turning slowly on its own axis to comprehend the whole pattern" (p. 248). Durrell (or Pursewarden) is of course not talking about *The Good Soldier* but about a book that is still to be done, yet what he says describes Ford's novel of forty years before.

The series of repeating dates serves then as an axis, a still point about which the book slowly turns—or it is like a cracked disk, a single moment that repeats itself endlesly. Why, though, August 4 rather than another date chosen at random? For Ford, August 4 was a date of very special importance, a day of infamy. On August 3, 1914, the world for him was still much the same familiar world that it had been on any date of any year before.

> But from the moment when, on the 4th of August, 1914, the Germans crossed the Belgian frontier "near a place called Gemmenich," aspects of the earth no longer existed for him.
>
> The earth existed, of course. Extending to immense distances of field-gray; dimly colored in singularly shaped masses, as if the colors on Mercator's projection had been nearly washed out by a wet brush. Stretching away, very flat, silenced, in suspense, the earth—*orbis terrarum veteribus notus*—seemed to await the oncoming legions, gray too, but with the shimmer of gold standards that should pour out from that little gap, "near a place called Gemmenich," and should obscure and put to shame all the green champaign lands of the world, as the green grass of meadows is put to shame and obscured by clay, water pouring through a gap in a dike. That was the earth.
>
> There were no nooks, no little, sweet corners; there were no assured homes, countries, provinces, kingdoms, or races. All the earth held its breath and waited.[30]

Nor is the above passage from *No Enemy* the only place where August 4, 1914, is mentioned by Ford. Indeed, the date seems to have an almost obsessive interest for him. Another postwar book, *Return to Yesterday*, ends on this note of ironic understatement:

[30] Ford Madox Ford, *No Enemy* (1929), pp. 21–22.

On the fourth of August the Northern Edition of *The Daily Mail* appeared with, on its placards:

Northern Boxing Competition
Morpeth Championship[31]

It is impossible, then, to believe that Ford's selection of his recurring date for *The Good Soldier* was a matter of chance merely, even though August 4, 1914, is not mentioned in the novel (the series ending exactly one year earlier), for all the futile wrigglings of the Dowells and Ashburnhams take place beneath its shadow.[32]

The little, hard fact that fecundated Ford's great auk's egg, the tiny germ from which it grew, was a scene of parting at which he had been present as an onlooker and which he describes in *The Spirit of the People* (1907). In its table of contents the incident is listed under the headings "The husband and the ward.—The repression of emotion.—The confronting of tragedies.—Playing the game." These might be subsumed under the one word "Silence."

The circumstances of this parting anticipate those of Edward's packing Nancy off to India. Like Dowell, Ford had been asked to drive to the station with the husband and his ward. At the leave-taking Ford observed with a fascinated and compassionate horror that there was not even a shaking of hands. The husband merely touched the visor of his cloth cap and, as the train pulled out, turned on his heel and walked through the ticket office to pick up a package of fish for lunch, got into his buggy, and drove off. Ford adds: "He had forgotten me —but he had kept his end up."[33]

[31] *Return to Yesterday*, p. 417.

[32] Candor compels me to acknowledge a major objection to this reading. It remains uncertain whether *The Good Soldier* was not already completed by August 4, 1914, even though it was not published until a year later. Indeed, in *Return to Yesterday* Ford says that by June, 1914, his novel was behind him. However, he was notoriously inaccurate in factual matters. The portion of the novel that was printed in the June, 1914, issue of *Blast* is early and does not include the "August 4" references. It proves nothing either way. I can only say that if Ford's August 4 and the Kaiser's were no more than a coincidence it is a stranger one than any in the book itself.

[33] See Ford Madox Hueffer, *England and the English: An Interpretation* (1907), pp. 338–339.

This account leaves considerable doubt as to the appropriate attitude to be taken toward the parting. On the one hand, he acknowledges that it was surely desirable "in the face of the eternal verities—the verities that bind and gather all nations and all creeds—" that the parting be complete and that it be arranged "decently." But that it should take place in "a silence so utter: a so demonstrative lack of tenderness" seemed to him a sign of a national characteristic that was "almost appalling." And yet, despite this insight, when Ford came to write *The Good Soldier* it was silence—reticence, even extreme taciturnity—that was to supply the standard by which each of his characters would be judged. Perhaps silence is golden precisely because speech is worth more than gold. One of the assumptions underlying most of Ford's writing is the desperate need of communication and the near impossibility of its attainment. Following long periods of silence or conventional chatter the need manifests itself, if sporadically. In *The Good Soldier* each of the main characters makes at some point a confession and, like Prufrock, attempts for once to tell all. Yet, paradoxically, this attempt at communication is successful only to the extent that the person confessing is by nature usually disinclined to make confessions, is reticent, passionate, and proud.

At the muddy bottom of the scale of those who tell all is the blabmouth, the person who speaks not out of the pressure of feeling but from sheer incontinences. There is, for example, the stranger named Bagshawe, who on seeing Florence in the lobby at Nauheim blurts out to her husband (not realizing that poor Dowell *is* her husband), "By Jove! Florry Hurlbird," adding that the last time he had seen her she was coming out of the bedroom of a young man named Jimmy at five o'clock in the morning. Compared with someone like this even a blackmailer seems virtuous, for he has at least a reason to be speaking—and speaks perhaps with shame.

As if to illustrate the point, Ford shows us a blackmailer in action. Dowell thinks of Major Basil, who had come upon some letters to his wife, and wonders how a blackmailer makes his demands. He conceives of the major as showing the letters to Edward with furious oaths, then accepting his explanation that the letters were perfectly innocent if the wrong construction were not put upon them. Then the major would say: "I say, old chap, I'm deuced hard up. Couldn't you lend me three hundred or so?" (p. 172) Yet, though more purposeful than the gossip, the major is rather like Bagshawe since he is not in Dowell's opinion really evil in any positive sense. The major, Dowell has discovered, collects different types of horses' bits from the earliest times but does not do even this with much vigor. Dowell sums him up with the words "He was a slack, loose, shiftless sort of fellow" (p. 165)—and therein apparently lies the major's lack of virtue.

Virtue, in Ford's somewhat old-fashioned view, is always silent where points of honor are concerned, even when this silence may contribute to the injury of an innocent victim—as, for example, Dowell himself. Thus the Misses Hurlbird, Florence's maiden aunts, do everything short of revealing her nature in order to save Dowell from the mistake of marrying Florence; yet at the critical point they do not give her away.

> They even, almost, said that marriage was a sacrament; but neither Miss Florence nor Miss Emily could quite bring herself to utter the word. And they almost brought themselves to say that Florence's early life had been characterized by flirtations—something of that sort.
>
> I know I ended the interview by saying:
>
> "I don't care. If Florence has robbed a bank I'm going to marry her and take her to Europe."
>
> And at that Miss Emily wailed and fainted. But Miss Florence, in spite of the state of her sister, threw herself on my neck and cried out:
>
> "Don't do it, John. Don't do it. You're a good young man," and she added, whilst I was getting out of the room to send Florence to her aunt's rescue:
>
> "We ought to tell you more. But she's our dear sister's child."
>
> Florence, I remember, received me with a chalk-pale face and the exclamation:
>
> "Have those old cats been saying anything against me?" (pp. 81–82)

This brings us to Florence, who has her finger in the dike with respect to the secret of her own infidelities and Edward's and takes a perverse pleasure in slowly pulling it out. Florence is the most nearly depraved person in the book; like Bagshawe (her appropriate nemesis) she tells all, wantonly, for no reason. And she infects others, Leonora in particular.

It appears that Florence was in two minds whether to confess to me or to Leonora. Confess she had to. And she pitched at last on Leonora, because if it had been me she would have had to confess a great deal more. Or, at least, I might have guessed a great deal more, about her "heart," and about Jimmy. So she went to Leonora one day and began hinting and hinting. And she enraged Leonora to such an extent that at last Leonora said:

"You want to tell me that you are Edward's mistress. You can be. I have no use for him."

That was really a calamity for Leonora, because once started, there was no stopping the talking. She tried to stop—but it was not to be done. (pp. 191–192)

Dowell comments:

Florence was an unstoppable talker. You could not stop her; nothing would stop her. Edward and Leonora were at least proud and reserved people. Pride and reserve are not the only things in life; perhaps they are not even the best things. But, if they happen to be your particular virtues you will go all to pieces if you let them go. And Leonora let them go. (p. 185)

By a chain reaction, Leonora's loss of reticence is in turn extended to Nancy, to Edward, and eventually possibly even to Dowell, too, if we are to think of him as whispering his saddest story into the beguiled reader's ear. We are told of Leonora and Nancy: "And they sat, crouching together in each other's arms, and crying and crying; and they lay down in the same bed, talking and talking, all through the night. And all through the night Edward could hear their voices through the wall. That was how it went" (p. 232).

And yet silence is not to be balked so easily. This unraveling of an ordered world in speech is disturbing, but doubly disturbing in that its insane insistence points in turn to another kind of silence, not reticence, but the void, the vacuum that is at the center of all the talk and that the talk in vain tries to hide: *nada, le néant*, the deep blankness of Archibald MacLeish's "nothing, nothing, nothing—nothing at all."

In the early nineteen-thirties describing the postwar years, Ford wrote in *It Was the Nightingale*: "In the old days we had seemed to have ourselves and our destinies well in hand. Now we were drifting towards a weir." He added that all who had taken part in the War were by its completion "mad"; for them the familiar landmarks of the world, the houses and busses, no longer seemed to be—really—houses and busses. He had seen too many of them gutted and smashed. Ford understood this fall from innocence of a generation as the consequence of a shattering revelation: "It had been revealed to you that beneath Ordered Life itself was stretched the merest film with, beneath it, the abysses of Chaos. One had come from the frail shelters of the Line to a world that was more frail than any canvas hut."[34]

This is much the world that Dowell is left with following his private fall from innocence (or ignorance) and against whose complete acceptance he continues to struggle rather dazedly. The objects of that world have the vividness of unreality. "And I thought nothing; absolutely nothing. I had no ideas; I had no strength. I felt no sorrow, no desire for action, no inclination to go upstairs and fall upon the body of my wife. I just saw the pink effulgence, the cane tables, the palms, the globular match-holders, the indented ashtrays" (p. 108). Later, he clutches his figure of the ordered and harmonious past seen as a minuet and tries to persuade himself that the past—at least *as past*—is indestructible. "The mob may sack Versailles; the Trianon may fall, but surely the minuet—the minuet itself is dancing itself away into the furthest stars" (p. 6). Yet in the act of developing the figure Dowell admits bitterly that the figure is false. The sanatorium at Bad Nauheim was in fact no setting for a minuet; rather "it was a prison—a prison full of screaming hysterics, tied down so that they might not outsound the rolling of our carriage wheels as we went along the shaded avenues of the Taunus Wald" (p. 7). This is a horrifying discovery; it is as though Dowell were forced to anticipate in miniature the experience reserved a year later for the 1914 generation in the trenches. Indeed, the ratio between the two experiences is suggested when he remarks early:

You may well ask why I write. And yet my reasons are quite many. For it is not unusual in human beings who have witnessed the sack of a city or

[34] Ford Madox Ford, *It Was the Nightingale* (1933), pp. 63–64.

the falling to pieces of a people to desire to set down what they have witnessed for the benefit of unknown heirs or of generations infinitely remote; or, if you please, just to get the sight out of their heads.

Someone has said that the death of a mouse from cancer is the whole sack of Rome by the Goths, and I swear to you that the breaking up of our little four-square coterie was such another unthinkable event. (p. 5)

The impending breakup, the expected sack of Rome, the madness to come is cunningly worked into the texture of the narrative in a variety of ways, some peculiarly verbal. One word in particular deserves note. Like King Lear or Hamlet, Jean-Paul Sartre, Mr. MacLeish, and Hemingway's old waiter, Dowell is haunted by nothingness. The word "nothing" keeps rising to the surface in his utterances, in part perhaps because it is a word with an extraordinarily wide range of contexts, pairing easily with other words to suggest at one extreme triviality ("such nothings") and standing for utter annihilation at the other. For that matter, it might appear often in anyone's prose. "Nothing" enters into the idea of innocence ("know nothing"), of deliberate silence ("say nothing"), of health ("nothing the matter with"), of refusal ("nothing doing"), and of a leisured way of life ("do nothing"). The word turns up frequently in *The Good Soldier* in conventional, nearly meaningless turns of phrase ("nothing less than," "nothing I like better than," "nothing to the point") that perhaps tend to inure us to its ultimate ontological mysteriousness as the opposite of something, the vacuum nature abhors and the limbo God permits.

The first deliberate use of the word comes early, in Dowell's confession to a kind of social agnosticism: "I know nothing—nothing in the world—of the hearts of men. I know only that I am alone—horribly alone" (p. 7). In much the same context, it appears again a few pages later, together with one of its two familiar opposites, "everything."

Is the whole thing a folly and a mockery? . . .

I don't know. And there is nothing to guide us. And if everything is so nebulous about a matter as elementary as the morals of sex, what is there to guide us in the more subtle morality of all other personal contacts, associations, and activities? Or are we meant to act on impulse alone? It is all a darkness. (p. 12)

Yet it is a fertile darkness; "nothing" can be a source of dismay, but also of wonder: the borderline between nothing and something (like the Iron Curtain) is probably equally mysterious when crossed from either direction. So a man speaks to a girl and finds only after speaking that he is hopelessly in love: "It was as if his passion for her hadn't existed; as if the very words that he spoke, without knowing that he spoke them, created the passion as they went along. Before he spoke, there was nothing; afterwards, it was the integral fact of his life" (p. 116). It is probably largely because of such uses as these (and other examples could be added) that certain key passages in which "nothing" appears have such an eerie resonance. For example:

You ask how it feels to be a deceived husband. Just Heavens, I do not know. It feels like just nothing at all. It is not Hell, certainly it is not necessarily Heaven. So I suppose it is the intermediate stage. What do they call it? Limbo. No, I feel nothing at all about that. They [Florence and Edward] are dead; they have gone before their Judge who, I hope, will open to them the springs of His compassion. It is not my business to think about it. (p. 70)

Dowell's mind moves dispiritedly from "Just Heavens" to "just nothing." The "intermediate stage" that he refers to one would suppose might be Purgatory, though not surprisingly Dowell does not seem able to recall this. He is close to the imbecile center of *nada* with his odd *non sequitur* "certainly it is not necessarily Heaven" and apparently quite blind when he says "it is not my business to think about it" and then proceeds to think about little else. "Nothing at all," appearing twice, has here very nearly its full force as the familiar name of the incurable split (Humpty Dumpty's tragic flaw) that is at the heart of existence, being related to its modest opposite "something" (its immodest opposite would be "everything") as silence is to speech. The abyss of *nada*, however, is ultimately no verbal matter, for the abyss denies all words and is, like the Godhead, ineffable, though it can be suggested when speech points to the opposed mystery of silence, a puzzle for all, but especially for the writer who lives by words.

In *The Good Soldier* the deepest silence comes late, in the insane quiet of Nancy's almost catatonic stillness—which is so much more appalling than if she were to rave *à la* Ophelia. Nancy here takes her place in a line of Fordian mutes that begins with the mad vicar in *The Benefactor* (1905), extends through *A Call* (1910)—with its fey little girl who won't talk and the guilty young man, a friend of her uncle's, who is unable to talk after picking up a ringing telephone in a strange house in the wee hours and realizing that his voice has been recognized—on through to the apoplectic Mark Tietjens dying in his lean-to shelter in *The Last Post* (1928), and perhaps beyond.

Ford's mutes seem nearer the heart of things than the wordy creatures around them, though whether the heart of things more fully partakes of heaven or of hell is, as we have seen, not always easy to say. For that matter, at the center of most of Ford's writing is silence, whether the still point of his lyric verse—

Out of the window [of the train] I see a dozen great stars, burning bright,
Flying in silence . . .[35]

—or such a quiet interlude as the following from *The Good Soldier*:

Edward was lounging in his chair smoking a cigar and he said nothing for quite five minutes. The candles glowed in the green shades; the reflections were green in the glasses of the bookcases that held guns and fishing-rods. Over the mantelpiece was the brownish picture of the white horse. Those were the quietest moments that I have ever known. (p. 249)

But usually in Ford's universe (however it may be in the greater one outside his books) the silence of the abyss proves to be the deeper and more real. The pleasant lyric quiet usually has something of the illusory, even the fraudulent, about it, as when these quietest moments that Dowell has ever known are followed immediately by Edward's jolting all-night confession.

For the purest examples of the deeper silence the reader must turn to Ford's writing about war, in particular to scenes in *Parade's End* where the roar of bombardment finally registers on the amazed and outraged eardrum less as noise than as what Ford calls, beautifully, "a rushing silence.":

After its mortal vomiting all the other sounds appeared a rushing silence, painful to ears in which the blood audibly coursed. The young officer stood

[35] Ford Madox Hueffer, "In the Train," *Collected Poems* (1914), p. 55.

violently up on his feet and caught at the complications of his belt hung from a nail. The elder, across the table, lounging sideways, stretched out one hand with a downwards movement. He was aware that the younger man, who was the senior officer, was just upon out of his mind. The younger man, intolerably fatigued, spoke sharp, injurious, inaudible words, to his companion. The elder spoke sharp, short words, inaudible too, and continued to motion downwards with his hand over the table. (p. 293)

In *The Good Soldier*, however, there is no rushing silence. Nancy's awful stillness is regarded entirely from the outside—and, besides, it is not complete. Ford does not take us into the abyss; we are brought to the edge, invited to look in and then are permitted to withdraw.

This incompleteness is in keeping with the novel's stasis, and it is an aspect of the story's sadness: "I call this the Saddest Story rather than 'The Ashburnham Tragedy,' just because it is so sad, just because there was no current to draw things along to a swift and inevitable end" (p. 164).

I think Dowell is right. His story is sadder than tragedy. In the threat of total annihilation and war's rushing silence there is something at least potentially purifying akin to the meaning of total darkness in the poems of T.S. Eliot—or St. John of the Cross's dark night of the soul—as opposed to twilight uncertainties, the "twittering world." Nancy's is a twittering world. At her craziest she is always tractable and socially correct: "Even when she was mad Nancy could behave herself" (p. 235). To see her, still beautiful and still beautifully dressed, one would hardly suppose, we are told, that anything serious was amiss. Sadder and more horrible than her silence, even, is Nancy's travesty of a recovery, the note upon which the action of this, Ford's most despairing, novel ends:

Once, or perhaps twice, during the meal her knife and fork will be suspended in mid-air as if she were trying to think of something that she had forgotten. Then she will say that she believes in an Omnipotent Deity or she will utter the one word, "shuttlecocks," perhaps. It is very extraordinary to see the perfect flush of health on her cheeks, to see the lustre of her coiled black hair, the poise of the head upon the neck, the grace of the white hands—and to think that it all means nothing. (p. 254)

iv. THE WAR AS FAIRY TALE

> *That Ford was almost an* hallucine *few of his intimates can doubt. . . . [He] saw quite distinctly the Venus immortal crossing the tram tracks.*
>
> —Ezra Pound

Since it is all too easy to exaggerate particular influences, the preceding chapter requires a certain corrective, for if Ford's technique and his sympathies were largely French, his temperament, personality, and prevailing tweedy persona were not. He tells us that when he spoke French he tried to speak correctly but with a deliberate English accent, to remind his auditors that he was, after all, an English gentleman. I suppose we should have to call Ford's temperament Anglo-Teutonic. He might not have liked that.

Not having known Ford personally, I have in mind the temperament revealed by the writing—of a somewhat wheezy, sometimes rather sentimental fabulist, the teller of marvelous fairy tales. Yet, in the telling, temperament and technique tend to become one. In certain respects *The Good Soldier* is not typical of Ford's novels, for though committed in theory to rendering his day strictly in terms of his day, to piling up and arranging little slices of life, Ford was in fact about as erring a realist as can be imagined.

His early fiction in particular covers an odd variety of subjects: an invasion from the Fourth Dimension, the strange behavior of two giants who live at a German sanitarium, a descent of the god Apollo on Edwardian London, enchantment of a vigilant knight by the White

Goddess, witchcraft, and several queer penetrations into the past. These fantasies, existing somewhere in a middle ground between the whimsical and the weird, Ford dismissed as *tours de force*,[1] yet they make up the bulk of his fictional writing and were essential (though Ford may not have seen this) to the few novels of modern life where he was to triumph on his own terms. In such fantasies as *Ladies Whose Bright Eyes* or *The Young Lovell*, Ford explored an aspect of experience that otherwise he could not have approached, what I shall call the fairy-tale aspect. And without it his realism would have been impoverished. It is an aspect present in all Ford's best work, a strangeness in the texture of things, as though he were looking at a perfectly workaday scene (of busses and bugs and bicycles) through stereoscopic glasses, with one lens focussed upon the familiar, even the banal, and the other upon the world of the fairies. This is especially true of *Parade's End*, the most stereoscopic of his books.

The chief influence—certainly the chief foreign influence—upon both Conrad and Ford was, as we have seen, the tradition of the French realists extending through Maupassant and Flaubert back to Stendhal, writers who had raised novel writing to an art not by being more gifted than their English contemporaries but by taking the novel more seriously. In that respect they were admirable; but, unfortunately, to be held serious in their day the novel, like other forms of art, was expected to compete with science largely upon its own terms. It must "constater" (as Ford was fond of saying), it must record things as they are. Though Ford accepted the aim, it was something he was temperamentally unable to fulfill (in the narrow sense in which they and he defined it), since to record things as they are is not only often to ratify things as they are, it is usually to insist on their "thingyness"; to turn whatever is, whether person or place, into a thing—to render it static.

The point can be illustrated with the familiar example of Emma Bovary. As the offspring of nineteenth-century science Flaubert's realism was determinist with a vengeance. Given his heroine's particular education and economic status, her good looks, her doting father, plus an environment with men like Charles, Léon, and Rodolphe in it, and

[1] See Dedicatory Letter, Ford Madox Ford, *The Good Soldier* (1951), p. xviii.

the rest—the adulteries, extravagances, selfishnesses, despair—follows remorselessly. As a free agent Emma is not only less real and believable than, say, Hamlet or Roskolnikov, whose creators held beliefs that went beyond the confines of scientific realism; she is less real than Cinderella. She is enslaved to three things: to a failure of communication, to the remorselessness of time, and to her own (bourgeois) identity. Emma never understands Charles nor is understood by him or Rodolphe: her pursuit of love is itself a desperate attempt to communicate—doomed from the start. It is a pursuit that takes time, and time is for Emma the enemy. Time is a one-way street, since for the realist hero or heroine there is no turning back and little looking around: Emma is in all respects time's victim, never its master. As a result, her very identity is a trap. The realist hero can never change, for to change, other than superficially, a human being must take stock of himself; but to grant that he can take stock of himself—has in fact been continually taking stock of himself since about the age of five—is to undermine the whole deterministic structure upon which realism rests. Emma never takes stock, never accepts responsibility for her own identity or for anything else—not even, I think, in the horrible moment of truth upon her deathbed.

In the fairy world of Alice, Goldilocks, and Cinderella it is quite otherwise. There communication never fails. In fairy tales there may be deliberate deception (the grandmotherly wolf misleading Red Ridinghood) but there is never the frustration of semantic blockage: when the characters say what they mean they are understood. Nor is communication limited to other human beings; the heroes—and also the villains—of fairy tale can often communicate with animals, plants, inanimate objects, and so on ("Mirror, mirror, on the wall . . ."). And when physically separated, they can communicate through spells. Also, as regards time, they are much freer than the Emma Bovarys: in fairy tales one can revisit the past and explore the future. Indeed, time in fairy tales is often relative. Edwin Sidney Hartland has commented upon "the supernatural lapse of time in fairyland"[2] and has brought to light many variations upon the familiar situation of Rip Van Winkle, where a minute spent by a human visitor in fairy-

[2] See Edwin Sidney Hartland, *The Science of Fairy Tales: An Inquiry into Fairy Mythology* (London: Walter Scott, 1897), Chs. VII–IX.

land may correspond to a year gone by on earth or, conversely, in some tales a year spent in fairyland takes away only a minute from the visitor's human life. Finally, as regards identity, in fairy tales it is the most fluid thing imaginable, since metamorphosis is the rule, not the exception: a serving girl may become a princess, a pumpkin become a coach, or a frog become a handsome prince—may, and probably will. The import of this is evident: identity is mysterious, volatile, not something easily delineated or defined.

Ford, as I see it, was committed by intellect to deterministic realism—but some part of him was not committed. He wrote his various fantasies and went on worrying about the great realistic novel that he was going, some day, to write. Apparently he saw no connection between the two activities and never recognized that without these *pastiches* and *tours de force* behind him he would have been unable to define his subject or develop it. More than most, Ford needed to come to reality by way of fantasy: "Giants first, then giants and generals" would have been the formula. But before looking for the giants and fairies—and the generals—in *Parade's End*, let us examine briefly three of these earlier and distinctly odder fictions.

2

The "Half Moon" (1909) is a novel of possession and unholy communion. Its heroine-villainess or villainess-heroine is a seventeenth-century witch named Anne Jeal, who is a Roman Catholic, devout in her fashion, but passionate and quite unscrupulous. The old religion, as old religions are apt to do in times of enforced change, has gone underground and survives for Anne not as sacrament but as magic. Her witchcraft is put to the service of love, for Anne is the jilted mistress of a local sailor (Edward Colman) who prefers her placid Protestant rival (Magdalena Kooch)—though he has named his small coaster for Anne. Anne trusts in her witchcraft to get Colman back, or, failing that, at least *to make him feel her*. If necessary, she will destroy him.

She fashions patiently a little man of wax and works up some other spells. Her former lover, meanwhile, has left Rye and has signed on with Henry Hudson for the trip to the New World. There follows a more or less accurate account of a long ocean passage (Ford is in this respect no Joseph Conrad) much beset by storms and head winds. The storms are, of course, not entirely natural, since they emanate from Anne and her evil spells. But it is the effigy that is her principal bond. It links her to Edward Colman as a remembrancer, and on occasion it can be useful.

Once, when she had been unable to bear never hearing his voice she had sweated it a little before a fire . . . and she had heard his voice then, uttering the words, "*I believe this is death coming to me*!"

This sweating she had done, not to harm him so much as from shear longing to hear his voice. It was unbearable not to do it when she had always that remedy. But she carried the image always with her, beneath her farthingale or between her breasts, for she was afraid that, if she let it out of her keeping, by some mischance it might break, and so he would die.[3]

Of course, eventually Anne overdoes it; and of course eventually she reaches the limits of her patience and her jealousy of Magdalena Kooch prevails: she puts the little man to death. But this murder is a kind of consummation. Though Magdalena stolidly believes her love is the stronger, Anne's appears to be the closer union. She shares in Colman's death agony, seeing and hearing him across the Atlantic, just as dying he sees and hears her.

Ladies Whose Bright Eyes (1911) is, par excellence, a time-fantasy. The story is somewhat as follows. A prosperous English publisher, Mr. Sorrell, is on his way to London when, near Salisbury, his train goes off the rails. Mr. Sorrell loses consciousness and when he regains it finds himself dressed in a sort of hospital nightshirt wandering through a strange landscape that is both England and not England. He recognizes Salisbury Cathedral, but otherwise no place could seem more foreign. He is hailed by the people he meets (even more strangely dressed) as a holy man come from the East whose arrival has long been expected. He discovers that these people think the time is the early fourteenth century. Apparently it is. At first Mr. Sorrell is appalled by the disease, filth, and beggars he encounters

[3] Ford Madox Hueffer, *The "Half Moon"* (1909), pp. 328–329.

everywhere—also by the medieval food—but slowly he comes to admire the chivalry and courtesy of the age.

Time passes, apparently many months. He is knighted, he falls in love; indeed two armed ladies fight in the lists for his hand. But all the while a new strangeness is added to all this strangeness: Mr. Sorrell (now Sir William) hears an odd insistent drilling and is haunted at moments by presences and half-presences. And then on one occasion in springtime when he is reclining in a flowered mead with his lady love, he suddenly smells chloroform! It is with difficulty that he struggles back to her and to the fourteenth century—though he does, but not before he is granted the germ of the following reflection:

> Was it possible that the ages superimposed themselves the one over the other? That they co-existed? Why not? . . . The half minute last past was now as dead as any half minute of a thousand years ago. As dead; but no more dead: as irrevocable, but no more irrevocable. Then why not as immortal?
>
> Yes, they co-existed. It was perhaps only the human perception that could not appreciate co-existing scenes. Though you can of course. You can look at thin mist and see the mist or you can equally look through the mist and see the sun.[4]

When, shortly, he wakes in a hospital room, once again in the twentieth century, he learns that only a few days have passed since the train wreck. England is superficially as he had left it; but, like all visitors to fairyland, when he returns to his own place and time Mr. Sorrell is a changed man.

The Brown Owl (1892) is a Victorian fairy tale pure and simple, and Ford's first book. It is about a King who was metamorphosed into an owl. There was once upon a time a beautiful Princess who was the daughter of a great magician, King at a court of magicians. The King was very good, but certain of his court were very bad, particularly his gloomy prime minister, by name Merrymineral. The King, having remained on the throne for nine hundred ninety-nine and one-half years, told his young daughter one day that he must soon depart but adjured her to trust the Owl—though as yet there was no owl to trust.

[4] Ford Madox Ford, *Ladies Whose Bright Eyes* (1935), pp. 302–303. These reflections are left implicit in the 1911 (London) edition.

There soon was, however, and the King was soon gone. The Owl proved to be a remarkable bird; it could change its size at will, sometimes perching on the Princess's shoulder and sometimes transporting her through the air on its back. How remarkable it was the wicked Prime Minister was soon to discover: to try out his own powers Merrymineral turned three pages who were still loyal to the Princess into water rats, but the Owl immediately turned them back into pages.

So things continued for some time, a cold war among the magicians until at last open hostilities broke out between those loyal to the Princess and the henchmen of the evil Prime Minister. A handsome Prince came to lead the forces of right, but unaided he was no match for Merrymineral. In the end it was the Owl who turned the tide in the Princess's favor. The Prime Minister was totally routed and ultimately irreversibly transmogrified, bursting into flame and ascending from sight like a fire balloon. At this point the Owl reassumed the shape of the Princess's father. Of course, the Princess married the handsome Prince, and both lived happily forever after.

3

In *Parade's End* these early experiments that looked like entertainments finally paid off. No one has ever written about modern trench warfare out of a more peculiar background. Though depicting life in the trenches, Ford treated the trenches as though they were fairyland; and, strangely, they came alive and stayed alive.

Christopher Tietjens visits the front as Mr. Sorrell visited the fourteenth century, and when he comes back both he and England are changed. *Parade's End* is a great slow novel of change: social, psychological, normative. Above all, it is a novel of qualitative change, a change in the way of *seeing* things, brought on by—or through—the First World War. From the thirties looking back, Ford wrote of the period immediately following the Armistice (in a passage that was cited earlier):

> No one could have come through that shattering experience and still view life and mankind with any normal vision. In those days you saw objects that the earlier mind labelled as *houses*. They had been used to seem cubic and solid permanences. But we had seen Ploegsteert where it had been re-

vealed that men's dwellings were thin shells that could be crushed as walnuts are crushed. . . . Nay, it had been revealed to you that beneath Ordered Life itself was stretched the merest film with, beneath it, the abysses of Chaos. One had come from the frail shelters of the Line to a world that was more frail than any canvas hut.[5]

Parade's End is a novel rendering such an experience. The first volume, *Some Do Not*, begins by evoking beautifully the bric-a-brac of Edwardian England, among which Ford's protagonist Christopher Tietjens, career man in a government office and son of a Yorkshire squire, moves heavily—away from his beautiful but unfaithful wife Sylvia and blunderingly toward a rather mousy young suffragette, Valentine Wannop. War breaks. In Volume Two, *No More Parades*, Ford takes us to a great replacement depot in France, where the "shattering experience" begins to affect what at the start of the novel had been Tietjens' almost excessively "normal vision." The third volume, *A Man Could Stand Up*, takes Tietjens into the trenches, the place of crushed walnuts, and brings him out again "mad," or at least gassed and shell-shocked, and leaves him on Armistice Day with Valentine Wannop in an empty house. The fourth volume, *The Last Post*, is a brief coda concerning the events of approximately one hour, some months later.

In Ford's renderings of the battle line the sense of Ordered Life resting upon a thin film, with Chaos under it, is evoked in various ways, some of a more or less literal or scenic sort: mining and countermining, for example. At the front, heaven knows what is under you. At one point Tietjens, himself in a wine cellar, sits up in his cot and listens to pickaxes deep below him (whether German or English he cannot say). He reflects that there may be others too, countermining, below them. For the most part, the sense of hollowness is evoked by other, less obvious, means. Confronting early morning in the trenches Tietjens mused: "This was like a nightmare," and then added quickly: "No it wasn't. It was like fever when things appear stiffly unreal. . . . And exaggeratedly real! Stereoscopic, you might say!" (p. 589) That exactly describes Ford's effect. The war scene is grim and terrible, with death at the center of it, but it is also sometimes strangely beau-

[5] Ford Madox Ford, *It Was the Nightingale* (1933) pp. 63–64.

tiful—a dematerialized and fairy world. So we have Tietjens looking over the parapet one early morning, following an artillery bombardment:

There were still the three wheels a-tilt, attached to slanting axles: in a haze of disintegrated wire, that, bedewed, made profuse patterns like frost on a window. . . . How the deuce had it not been *all* mashed to pieces by the last Hun barrage? Yet there were three frosty erections—like fairy sheds, half-way between the two lines. And, suspended in them, as there would have to be, three bundles of rags and what appeared to be a very large, squashed crow. How the devil had that fellow managed to get smashed into that shape? (p. 552)

At other times the fairy-tale quality of the front lines takes the form of a more domesticated, and withal a more subterranean, queerness:

The Rag Time Army: at its vocation: living and breathing.

The Sergeant called them to attention and they wavered back and forward. The Sergeant said:

"The Commandin' Officer's lookin' at you. *Fix* . . . B'ts!"

And, positively, a dwarf concealed under a pudding basin shuffled a foot-length and a half forward in the mud, protruded his rifle-muzzle between his bent knees, jerked his head swiftly to strain his sight along the minute line. . . . It was like a blurred fairy-tale! (p. 571)

From one point of view the experience in the trenches is regression: an adult returned to the infantile world of gnomes and ogres. Tietjens' state of mind is not healthy, as Ford well knew. By 1918, Ford believed, "every one who had taken physical part in the war was then mad."[6] Ford himself suffered a serious mental breakdown in France, as does Tietjens also. And yet from another point of view the hallucinated experience of the trenches amounts to a deeper insight where breakdown and breakthrough are one.

It is principally a matter of walls going down. In one of his reminiscences Ford tells of working through a long afternoon upon an outside wall in an old stone cottage on the coast of England. A window had been needed. When finally the work was over and the last stone removed, Ford looked up and saw through the framed empty space, clear and a little pink in the setting sun, the coast of France. It was,

[6] *Ibid.*, p. 63.

he said, a queer feeling: to be indoors in England and then to look up and see France. Though no more than another country glimpsed unexpectedly, the anecdote suggests a further and more shattering penetration into the timeless world through the looking glass, behind the mirror which the weary realist is expected to hold up to nature. Ford may have had such an experience in mind when he caused Mr. Sorrell to observe that we might look at the mist or we might look *through* the mist at the sun. Sister Bernetta Quinn in *The Metamorphic Tradition in Modern Poetry* speaks of perfection "longing to break through the façade of the quotidian"[7] and sees metamorphosis, which slides the façade away, as the means perfection uses. So, with respect to the phenomenal world, we may look at tables and chairs or we may look through them. At what? At whatever there is beyond, at the gods.

In an obituary notice in *Furioso*, Ezra Pound made the comment that I have taken as epigraph for this chapter: "That Ford was almost an *hallucine* few of his intimates can doubt. . . . [He] saw quite distinctly the Venus immortal crossing the tram tracks."[8] William Carlos Williams in a poem in the same issue called Ford "a heavenly man. . . , never having been for me a saintly one."[9] Ford had a somewhat different way of putting it. He was fond of repeating what he insisted was a Chinese proverb (it may or may not have been): "It would be hypocrisy to seek for the person of the Sacred Emperor in a low teahouse."[10] But he added that it was a bad proverb, since there was almost no other occupation worth pursuing.

Is there, then, in *Parade's End* some Sacred Emperor or Venus immortal? And if so, perceived by whom? And if the novel represents a transcendence or "breakthrough," then whose? Tietjens? Or Tietjens' and the author's? Probably both. For Tietjens, the slow ordeal of which his experience in the trenches is the outward and visible sign is a matter of sloughing off a false—or a superficial—identity and, in

[7] Sister M. Bernetta Quinn, *The Metamorphic Tradition in Modern Poetry* (New Brunswick, N.J.: Rutgers University Press, 1955), p. 4.

[8] Ezra Pound, "Ford Madox (Hueffer) Ford; Obit," *Furioso*, I, No. 3 (Spring, 1940), 2.

[9] William Carlos Williams, "To Ford Madox Ford in Heaven," *Furioso*, I, No. 3 (Spring, 1940), 4.

[10] See Ford Madox Ford, *Thus To Revisit* (1921), pp. 179 ff.

his resulting nakedness and dispossession, finding what Alan Watts would call his *supreme identity*.[11] For Ford, recording this process was at last a chance to have his fantasy and his realism together, since he had found a situation where fantasy equalled realism. In writing about the blowing up of parapets by heavy-caliber German artillery, about mud, mist, strafes, going over the top, and so on, and also in writing about the influences at home that were being mysteriously exerted upon the fate of the men in the trenches, Ford discovered he could have his fill of the uncanny, in particular these: witchcraft, strange penetrations into time past, and metamorphosis.

1. *Witchcraft*. Sylvia here is the wicked witch, who at the start with other "silly, idle girls" has been "playing at black masses"—not that this in itself means much. As her mother's friend Father Consett explains: "It's not much more than palmistry or fortune-telling to them if one has to weigh it, for all its ugliness, as a sin. As far as their volition goes, and it's volition that's the essence of prayer, black or white" (p. 42). The Father is doubtless right as far as the black masses are concerned; yet Sylvia is essentially a witch for all that. Father Consett, presumably not having read *The "Half Moon,"* does not know about Anne Jeal and her witcheries and so cannot see, as we can, that Sylvia is her spiritual offspring.

Passion with Sylvia, as with Anne, is a matter of *odi et amo*. Sylvia hates Tietjens and craves him. Her reasons for hate are diverse: because she had been pregnant when she married him and did not even know the father of her child; because he appeared willing to forgive her for this; and even more because he insists there is nothing to forgive. Perhaps most of all, Sylvia hates Tietjens because she loves him, because he alone seems to her a man in a world of adolescents. So at all costs he must be made to feel her. On one occasion when they are together she throws a salad plate in his direction and stains his tunic. That is not witchcraft. It is when they are apart that Sylvia's more demonic side is in evidence: she appears to be able to cast hate across the darkened wartime Channel and inflict suffering on her man by a

[11] See Alan W. Watts, *The Supreme Identity* (New York: The Noonday Press, 1957). "*Objective* knowledge of the Self is not only impossible but unnecessary. Properly understood, the Self is like light, which has no need to illumine itself because it is already luminous" (p. 48).

kind of remote control. It is here she most closely resembles Anne Jeal. In France, Tietjens is caused to have visions of her cruel, beautiful, and intense person:

He imagined hatred coming to him in waves from the convent in which Sylvia had immured herself. . . . He imagined Sylvia, coiled up on a convent bed. . . . Hating. . . . Her certainly glorious hair all round her. . . . Hating. . . . Slowly and coldly. . . . Like the head of a snake when you examined it. . . . Eyes motionless: mouth closed tight. (p. 339)

Or again:

She appeared before him so extraordinarily bright and clear in the brown darkness that he shuddered: very tall, very fair, extraordinarily fit and clean even. Thoroughbred! . . . She was looking straight before her, with a little inimical disturbance of the corner of her lips. She had just thought of a way to hurt terribly his silent personality. (p. 299)

This witchlike entente represents an advance in psychological perception for Ford, harrowing though it may be for his poor characters. It seems quite unlike anything in Flaubert or Maupassant, since one of the best things about Ford's treatment of the relations between the Tietjens is the impression he conveys of the extraordinary closeness of husband and wife, not in spite of the hate but, it would be almost truer to say, because of it. Sylvia and Christopher think the same thoughts, have the same visions, repeat the same jokes, and often say the same things. As Valentine Wannop ruefully observes of her rival: "She too had belonged to the Tietjens family and . . . had been intimate with their sayings to the point of saturation" (p. 826). I find this an original conception; and it seems likely that without the preliminary dip into witchcraft in *The "Half Moon"* this fresh vision of the perversities of human involvement could not have come about.

2. *Strange Penetrations into Time Past.* Here the gains are again both Tietjens' and the author's, yet not without pain. Tietjens' breakthrough comes by way of breakdown and dispossession, since near the front he is brought to see himself as obsolescent, at one point confessing resignedly to his godfather, General Campion: "I'm a Tory of such an extinct type that she [Sylvia] might take me for anything. The last megatherium" (p. 490). The megatherium is a huge, extinct, slothlike animal. Tietjens is like that. Though he gets more done than

most men, he characteristically moons along with his hands in his pockets and knows that his pace, his feeling for *noblesse oblige*, and his rather arbitrary sense of honor all put him at odds with most of those around him. As he also says, less resignedly: "It is not a good thing to belong to the seventeenth or eighteenth centuries in the twentieth" (p. 490). At the same time Tietjens comes into his own at the front, for the front, any front, is atavistic—or at least so strikes someone visiting it for the first time. How? This may take a little explaining.

Let us say that someone who had read the *Iliad* at an impressionable age, and had looked out toward the Greek camp from the ramparts of Troy, later, on finding himself upon, say, the Anzio Beachhead, would feel that he had been there before. Though methods of killing change, the atmosphere of death and danger does not. To visit the front is always to visit the past, and Ford evokes, as few other novelists have evoked, the archaic nature of a battlefield. As with the hospitalized publisher in *Ladies Whose Bright Eyes*, Tietjens in his crackup (though here it is a whole civilization that is wrecked and not an isolated train) is psychically liberated by breaking through the "thin film" that separates Ordered Life from Chaos. For, like Alice in her fall, it is less Chaos that is entered than Fairyland, a realm where time has been arrested and the past is still actual—where Humpty Dumpty still sits on his wall—and where anything may happen.

Ford has caught this queer battle atmosphere of time's arrest quite beautifully in several places, the opening of Chapter V of *A Man Could Stand Up* for example:

> The key-bugle remarked with singular distinctness to the dawn:
>
> *dy*
> *I know a la fair kind*
> *and*
> *Was never face*
> *so mind*
> *pleased my*
> *y*
>
> A sudden waft of pleasure at the seventeenth century air that the tones gave to the landscape went all over Tietjens. . . . Herrick and Purcell! . . . Or it was perhaps a modern imitation. Good enough. He asked:

"What the devil's that row, Sergeant?"

The Sergeant disappeared behind the muddied sacking curtain. There was a guard-room in there. The key-bugle said:

Fair *kind. . . .*
and
Fair *Fair* *Fair*
kind . . . .
and . . . *and . . .* *and* (p. 564)

It is like the moment of coexistence in *Ladies Whose Bright Eyes* when in the fourteenth-century field of love Mr. Sorrell suddenly smells chloroform—though it is the present rudely breaking into the past, there, while the past is beautifully and unexpectedly interpenetrating the present, here. In either case it is a moment outside time and is magical, in much the way that Eliot's moment in the rose garden is magical, or Proust's involuntary memory as he nods over his "madeleine" and tea.

The breakthrough into an enchanted realm, as I have said, seems to be both Tietjens' and Ford's. For Tietjens it is a moment of happiness in the midst of suffering, but also it is in the nature of a portent. Increasingly his half-conscious thoughts have been turning to the future and he has been moving toward a decision: that *après la guerre finit* (*if* he survives, and he believes he will) he will turn his back on London, with its government offices and overfurnished drawingrooms and women like Sylvia, and will live in the country with Valentine Wannop near some small seventeenth-century village resembling George Herbert's Bemerton—a name that keeps running through his head. For Ford too it is a consummation in that here his technical virtuosity in filtering the past through the present and the present through the past is perfectly relevant for once to a realistic treatment of the matter at hand.

3. *Metamorphosis.* Strictly speaking, there is no supernatural visitation in *Parade's End*, but there is at least a painful travesty of one, the arrival not of the Sacred Emperor but of a blinded, and dying, German:

The Hero arrived. Naturally, he was a Hun. He came over, all legs and arms going, like a catamount; struck the face of the parados, fell into the trench on the dead body, with his hands to his eyes, sprang up again and danced. With heavy deliberation Tietjens drew his great trench-knife rather than his revolver. Why? The butcher-instinct? Or trying to think himself with the Exmoor stag-hounds. The man's shoulders had come heavily on him as he had rebounded from the parados-face. He felt outraged. Watching that performing Hun he held the knife pointed and tried to think of the German for *Hands Up*. He imagined it to be *Hoch die Haende!* He looked for a nice spot in the Hun's side.

His excursion into a foreign tongue proved supererogatory. The German threw his arms abroad, his—considerably mashed!—face to the sky.

Always dramatic, Cousin Fritz! Too dramatic, really. (p. 559)

The characteristic real-unreal, stereoscopic effect is maintained from beginning to end. The action is a horrible farce; both Tietjens and the dying German are—or appear to be—play-acting. This impression is conveyed by means of the technical device of metamorphosis, though it is more than a technical device, since for Ford it represents a whole way of seeing. The grim passage is helped along by a series of small (farcical) metamorphoses: the German soldier changes rapidly from operatic Hero to catamount to wild dancer to dramatic ham actor; Tietjens changes from a whimsical reserve officer in the trenches to a gentleman hunter with the Exmoor hounds.

Quite close to the mood of Ford's early fairy tales—to the loyal pages in *The Brown Owl* who were changed into water rats—are other brief metamorphoses, in part for comic effect, that bring about minor transitions within a single long scene: "The sergeant-major, now a deferential shopwalker in a lady's store, pointed out that they had had urgent instructions . . ." (p. 324); "The sergeant-major, now a very important solicitor's most confidential clerk, began whispering to the colonel . . ." (p. 326), and so on. Closer still is what we might think of as totemistic metamorphosis, where (at least in the eyes of someone else) a character turns into the appropriate animal at the appropriate time. A good example is supplied by the following bit of high comedy, where General Campion has just been told by Sylvia that Tietjens "desires to model himself upon our Lord":

He said: "Good Lord! . . . Good Lord! . . . Of course his poor dear mother was a little . . . But, hang it! . . . The Wannop girl! . . ." Extreme discomfort overcame him. . . . Tietjens was half-way across the inner room, coming towards them.

He said:

"Major Thurston is looking for you, sir. Very urgently. . . ." The general regarded him as if he had been the unicorn of the royal arms, come alive. He exclaimed:

"Major Thurston! . . . Yes! Yes! . . ." and, Tietjens saying to him:

"I wanted to ask you, sir . . ." He pushed Tietjens away as if he dreaded an assault and went off with short, agitated steps. (p. 412)

Though they help control tone, the above metamorphoses are minor. The more important instances in *Parade's End* concern profound changes within the hero, or moments of self-discovery. Perhaps most important of all are transfigurations, epiphanies, moments when the here and now becomes preternaturally vivid and yet seems hardly to matter. War creates moods of this sort (as do funerals), when briefly, and oddly, the mortality of others serves to convince us of our own immortality. At such a time a man is poised between revelation and folly. The following passage suffers a little from being removed from its narrative context but will serve as an example. (It closely resembles a passage from *No Enemy* that was considered earlier.)

He had been coming down the reverse side of the range, feeling good. Probably because he had got out of that O.P. which the German guns had been trying to find. He went down with long strides, the tops of thistles brushing his hips. Obviously the thistles contained things that attracted flies. They are apt to after a famous victory. So myriads of swallows pursued him, swirling round and round him, their wings touching; for a matter of twenty yards all round and their wings brushing him and the tops of the thistles. And as the blue sky was reflected in the blue of their backs—for their backs were below his eyes—he had felt like a Greek God striding through the sea. (pp. 630–631)

At such a moment Tietjens very nearly *is* the Sacred Emperor. We recall that Sylvia has said of him to an embarrassed sergeant-major: "He saved others; himself he could not save" (p. 404). If it were not so fleeting, Christopher's feeling might be regarded as paranoid. In *Ladies Whose Bright Eyes*, when as a result of a train wreck Mr. Sorrell slipped into the past, he was transformed briefly into a knight; in *Parade's End* when Tietjens slips into a timeless realm as a result of a far greater wreck, he is turned for one long instant into a divinity.

4

Let us come back to the tables and chairs, to the quotidian facts of Ordered Life before its breakdown into Chaos. At the start of *Parade's End* there are too many tables and chairs, too much furnishings of every sort, overstuffed houses for overstuffed minds. Of the dining room of a prewar country parsonage we are told:

> The chairs, arranged along the long table that was set for eight people, had the delicate, spidery, mahogany backs of Chippendale; on the golden mahogany sideboard that had behind it green silk curtains on a brass-rail were displayed an immense, crumbed ham, more peaches on an epergne, a large meat-pie with a varnished crust, another epergne that supported the large pale globes of grapefruit; a galantine, a cube of inlaid meats, encased in thick jelly. (p. 80)

Breakfast is about to be served! It is these people's souls that are encased in thick jelly. Compare a postwar interior, the master bedroom of Tietjens' house from which all the furniture has been removed, making way for these articles:

> As if set down in a field, the room being so large, there camped. . . . A camp-bed for the use of officers, G.S. one, as the saying is. And implements of green canvas, supported on crossed white wood staves: a chair, a bucket with a rope handle, a washing-basin, a table. The bed was covered over with a flea-bag of brown wool. (p. 650)

And that is all. This is the bridal couch that Tietjens has prepared for himself and for Valentine Wannop, and she accepts it with good grace. She calls it "frugal and glorious."

Between these two interiors lies most of the action of the book. The latter scene is Tietjens' haven: years after meeting Valentine he has come through to her his true love. What had kept them apart was the furniture and all that the furniture represented: a leisured society that Ford in another book (*Return to Yesterday*) stigmatized as "fairly unavailing, materialist, emasculated—and doomed."

Tietjens' eventual union with Valentine Wannop was anticipated early in *Some Do Not* in the scene at dawn in the mist; but then no union was possible. The two had been helping Valentine's cosuffragette Gertie make her escape after a demonstration against government officials on a golf course. It was midsummer eve and nearly dawn, after an all night's ride behind a horse. Valentine had climbed down to see what she could see, and Tietjens nearly kissed her when she came up with her hair wet, as if from the sea—but refrained. Nothing came of it. Instead, General Campion's car emerged, monolithic and poorly driven, out of the fog and careened into them—bloodying their horse and anticipating in miniature the whole war. Later, after the outbreak of hostilities, Valentine and Christopher had further opportunities to become lovers, yet still did not. Some do not. But why? They loved each other and by that time Sylvia was no wife to Tietjens. They very nearly took the step on the eve of Tietjens' second going-out; but even then too many impediments of every sort still lay in the way.

Though the war was to be a great emptying, it had not had time yet to work its full effect upon them. Tietjens especially remained too much a part of the overstuffed Edwardian—or early Georgian—scene. He was still too vain of an encyclopedic knowledge, his head crammed with bric-a-brac of every sort. This omniscience was eventually to be lost in the trenches. On the first time out Tietjens suffered briefly complete amnesia, and though we find him back home on sick leave methodically reading through the *Encyclopaedia Britannica* in the attempt to regain lost knowledge, that side of his character is thereafter decreasingly in evidence. He turns more and more to poetry (which formerly he patronized rather contemptuously) and away from facts, as though in his mind the shale of an inherited clutter were dropping away to reveal strange surfaces previously unsuspected. At the end of *A Man Could Stand Up*, deprived of his inheritance, health, son, wife, facts, and good name—and having sold his beautiful furniture piecemeal—Tietjens at last can have his Valentine in a half-empty house. He has paid a heavy price: nearly everything.

In this union there is joy but also terror, a terror that is recorded for us by Valentine's shocked but passionate response to Christopher and the situation. She responds to him much as Tietjens has responded to the war: in terms of a fairy tale gone somewhat wobbly. The apparently half-mad Tietjens lurching downstairs with a cabinet under his arm (this is Valentine's first glimpse of him since the cessation of hostilities), his eyes bulging, his hair white, is no laughing matter—and inside the door, in the emptied house, Valentine is confronted with the pure chill of fairy tale. In her mind an image of Bluebeard rises to the surface, and when Tietjens returns shortly he is carrying a large sack:

The sack was the first thing she saw as he opened the door. Pushed it open; it was already half-open. A sack was a dreadful thing for a mad man to carry. In an empty house. He dumped the sack down on the hearth stone. He had coal dust on his right forehead. It was a heavy sack. Bluebeard would have had in it the corpse of his first wife. Borrow says that the gypsies say: "Never trust a young man with grey hair!" . . . He had only half-grey hair and he was only half young. He was panting. He must be stopped carrying heavy sacks. Panting like a fish. A great, motionless carp, hung in a tank. (p. 656)

For Valentine it is chill mixed with tenderness.

It is in the final scene of *A Man Could Stand Up* that Ford's long sojourn in the land of the giants and fairies is at last fully justified. Valentine's fear has not gone away; rather it is metamorphosed, transformed. In the saturnalia of Armistice Night during the general madness of rejoicing—in a scene that is scarcely naturalistic at all—the empty house slowly fills with the ghostlike figures of roisterers, one dying, one with but one eye, one with a monocle: Tietjens' comrades in arms, come back to tell him goodbye. There is music. Abruptly Valentine's fear is turned into wonder and joy—into amazement—as Tietjens, no longer a carp, undergoes for her a last and delightful metamorphosis:

They were going round them: yelling in unison:

"Over here! Pom Pom Over here! Pom Pom!
That's the word, that's the word; Over here. . . ."

At least they weren't over there! They were prancing. The whole world round them was yelling and prancing round. They were the centre of unending roaring circles. The man with the eye-glass had stuck a half-crown in his other eye. He was well-meaning. A brother. She had a brother with the V.C. All in the family.

Tietjens was stretching out his two hands from the waist. It was incomprehensible. His right hand was behind her back, his left in her right hand. She was frightened. She was amazed. Did you ever! He was swaying slowly. The elephant! They were dancing! Aranjuez was hanging on to the tall woman like a kid on a telegraph pole. The officer who had said he had picked up a little bit of fluff. . . . well, he had! He had run out and fetched it. It wore white cotton gloves and a flowered hat. It said: "Ow! Now!" . . . There was a fellow with a most beautiful voice. He led: better than a gramophone. Better. . . .

Les petites marionettes, font! font! font. . . .

On an elephant. A dear, meal-sack elephant. She was setting out on. . . . (pp. 673–674)

v. THE TIETJENS TRILOGY: A STEP BEYOND PARADE

"But if you marched a company into a field through a gateway and you wanted to get it out again but you did not know any command in the drill book for change of direction, what would you do, sir?"

—No More Parades

1. *Some Do Not*

In this chapter I hope to consolidate some of the ground occupied in the previous chapters by examining the Tietjens trilogy as to its import as a whole—and more particularly as to the development of the meaning of the affair from one volume to the next. Some repetition will be unavoidable. In *Parade's End* much comes together. Several of the elements that compose the vision of war that pervades the Tietjens books were found already in *No Enemy* and *The Marsden Case*, but there they were in isolation, insufficiently assimilated: the "French" prose, the motifs from fairy tale, the characteristic touch—but blurred, not properly "tuned in," as though Ford had not yet found his own wave length.

In his book on James, Ford remarks briefly on the psychology of shock, imagining how a man's mind operates when he discovers, for example, that he is about to be ruined: it is set in curious vibration. Let us suppose that you (the ruined man) are unable to stand the strain any longer in town and ask your best friend ("who won't be a friend any more to-morrow, human nature being what it is") to take a day off at golf with you. The friend accepts and off you go. Rather to your surprise you find yourself in remarkably good golfing form. The sky is blue, the day is fair.

> You joke about the hardness of the greens . . . You take your mashie and make the approach shot of your life whilst you are joking about the other fellow's necktie, and he says that if you play like that on the second of next month you will certainly take the club medal, though he knows, and you know, and they all know you know, that by the second of next month not a soul there will talk to you or play with you.

Ford concludes: "That, you know, is what life really is—a series of such meaningless episodes beneath the shadow of doom—or of impending bliss, if you prefer it." He adds: "And that is what Henry James gives you—an immense body of work all dominated with that vibration—with that balancing of the mind between the great outlines and the petty details."[1]

That is also the characteristic note of *Parade's End*, something almost Jamesian. No bayonets are thrust home with a grunt, no military obscenities are heard, no sudden brutalities are revealed, no hatred for sergeants and officers, or for the enemy; a complete chastity of thought and expression (of all surprising things for a war novelist) prevails throughout. The balancing mind juggles the various elements together—or say that a sudden crystallization produces many diamonds of pattern.

Ford has defined the subject of his "immense novel" or trilogy—for he called it both[2]—as "the world as it culminated in the war."[3] The world is a big place; ideally this subject should be developed, Ford felt, without individual characters—without golfers—but by an altogether different method.

> I sit frequently and dream of writing an immense novel in which all the characters should be great masses of people—or interests. You would have Interest A, remorselessly and under the stress of blind necessities, slowly or cataclysmically overwhelming Interest Z. Without the the attraction of sympathy for a picturesque or upright individual. It ought, I have felt for years, to be done. But I doubt if I shall ever get to it.[4]

[1] Ford Madox Hueffer, *Henry James: A Critical Study* (1913), pp. 154–155.

[2] It is both. So far as I know, he never called it his "tetralogy"; indeed Ford left directions (disregarded by the Knopf editor) that in the omnibus edition, to be called *Parade's End, The Last Post* should be omitted. Hence, we shall consider it separately.

[3] Ford Madox Ford, *It Was the Nightingale* (1933), p. 214.

[4] *Ibid.*, p. 215.

Instead he fell back upon a few memorable characters caught up in an interesting situation, or "affair"; and as for the "world" (or even a small part of it), it must be seen through the eyes of one of these characters who was to be a central observer thoroughly committed and involved: "The tribulations of the central observer must be sufficient to carry the reader through his observations of the crumbling world."

Ford tells us that he based Christopher Tietjens upon his old friend Arthur Marwood, who died before the War, though there must be a good deal of Ford in the portrait too, especially with respect to Tietjens' military service and his tribulations which are, if at all, only indirectly Marwoodian. Tietjens' picking up Sylvia on a train is apparently drawn from the life:

> We were going back to our cottages after a hard week over manuscripts in the office of the *English Review*. I said to Marwood:
>
> "What really became of Waring?"
>
> He said:
>
> "The poor devil, he picked up a bitch on a train between Calais and Paris. She persuaded him that he had got her with child. . . . He felt he had to marry her. . . . Then he found out that the child might be another man's, just as well as his. . . . There was no real knowing. . . . It was the hardest luck I ever heard of. . . . She was as unfaithful to him as a street walker. . . ."
>
> I said:
>
> "Couldn't he divorce?"
>
> —But he couldn't divorce. He held that a decent man could never divorce a woman. The woman on the other hand would not divorce him because she was a Roman Catholic.[5]

Waring's story (that was not his real name) is Tietjens'. His tribulations are not new when we first meet Tietjens on a train going down to Rye for a weekend of golf, but they have taken a new turn. He has had a shock, having learned that his wandering wife is coming back to him. The weekend makes matters worse, bringing added complications in the wake of Tietjens' befriending two young suffragettes who are bothering a cabinet minister on the golf course. The golf-course sequence is a rather richer variant of the hypothetical golfing

[5] *Ibid.*, pp. 209–210.

scene we have been imagining. It is the book's first substantial action following a panoramic assemblage of brief scenes which have served to build up the picture of a social world of some color and apparently some stability, and it beautifully reveals not merely the extent of Tietjens' troubles—these we already know something about—but the essential shakiness of an established order that in the opening pages had appeared to move as smoothly as the train taking Tietjens and his friend Macmaster down to Rye—as smoothly, Tietjens thought, "as British gilt-edged securities" (p. 3).

As he remarks the next day, "All sorts of bounders get into all sorts of holies of holies" (p. 94). He means even into his golf club. The bounders Tietjens has in mind are, first, "two men with bright green coats, red knitted waistcoats and florid faces" who are the weekend guests of the club and who are responsible for "an unpleasant chill in the air." They have been discussing subjects gentlemen do not discuss at a club; Tietjens' godfather, General Campion, has been called on to put them straight. Everyone is badly upset.

> "It makes one as beastly a bounder as themselves," he said. "But what the devil else was one to do?" The two city men had ambled hastily into the dressing-rooms; the dire silence fell. Macmaster realised that, for these Tories at least, this was really the end of the world. (p. 59)

It isn't quite, but it is a jolt.

It is soon followed by worse. As Tietjens' foursome are about to tee off one of them takes a bet offered by another gentleman (the cabinet minister, in fact) that one of his secretaries can "drive into and hit twice in eighteen holes the two city men who would be playing ahead of them"—which is not cricket or golf either. He very nearly does it too. But that is not the worst. More sacred for these Tories than golf even is the hunt, and before the afternoon is over it is travestied and degraded. For soon onto the golf course come the two suffragettes Valentine Wannop and Gertie Wilson (though Tietjens doesn't yet know their names), whereupon golf is dropped and the men—bounders, bystanders, and members of the Governing Class, together with a country constable—all set off after the girls. In this hunt, instead of foxes there are two young English ladies, and instead of foxhounds there is a breathy Member of Parliament (Tory) of whom we are told that he "was yelping just like a dog: 'Hi! Hi! Hi! Hi!' " By now there is no perceptible difference between the M.P. and the city men, one of whom continues shouting hilariously: "Strip the bitch naked! . . . Ugh . . . Strip the bitch stark naked!"

We realize at this point that all is not quite well in old England.

The episode on the golf course is the first of several encounters taking us through the remainder of the weekend. Tietjens and Valentine meet the next morning at the home of the local vicar for an astonishing—and astonishingly good—breakfast, which turns into a mad scene. This is followed by an assignation between Macmaster and the wife of the vicar, Mrs. Duchemin, a woman who has had much to put up with. It is in these strange and unpropitious circumstances that Valentine and Christopher fall in love, although no word is spoken—not even later in the mist on the all-night buggy ride when they are spiriting away Gertie Wilson to keep her out of the clutches of the local police. Part One of *Some Do Not* ends with that ride, with the sunrise that follows midsummer night, 1912. Part Two comprises a single day that is apparently in 1917 ("the third year of the war"), showing us Tietjens at home in London with his wife Sylvia (bored, in a plate-throwing mood); there is a visit from a banker who brings bad news, a look-in at the War Office, and several truncated scenes late that evening. After five years Christopher's love for Valentine is still undeclared, although it is mutually recognized; his growing tribulations are the consequence of this love and of his refusal to divorce Sylvia or even to defend himself from her slanders.

When his best motives continue to be misunderstood or twisted by those around him we become more and more aware of the crumbling social world, for Tietjens is a good man, and that he could be so consistently abused by his society (when he might rather be used) inclines us to doubt the soundness of that society. It seems to be Tietjens' principles that get him into trouble and keep him misunderstood. These principles are a curious blend of the conventional and the unconventional. It is a blend that causes him to appear inscrutable to such an *homme moyen sensuel* of the British upper classes as General Campion—an enigma, a "brilliant fellow" and hence, from the General's point of view, "unsound."

Sylvia, who is as much puzzled as any, remarks of her husband to a Catholic priest early in the story: "I tell you he's so formal he can't do without all the conventions there are and so truthful he can't use half of them" (p. 32). She has in mind a telegram he has just sent her where a letter would have been expected, in order to avoid beginning "Dear Sylvia." Instances of his fondness for his own conventions—his need for them—are numerous. There is a prescribed way of leaving a train (you must not stir until it has come to a standstill) and a prescribed way also of boarding, since last off implies last on, the privilege of rank: "Tietjens only caught the Rye train by running along side it, pitching his enormous kit-bag through the carriage window and swinging on the footboard. Macmaster reflected that if he had done that half the station would have been yelling, 'Stand away there' " (p. 22). Tietjens' conventions demand equally that he be unfailingly courteous to ladies, even when they resort to throwing things, and unfailingly patronizing if not downright rude to men. His French, when he speaks French, is grammatically correct and fluent but (like Ford's) spoken deliberately with an English accent "to show that he was an English county gentleman" (p. 408). He presents a wooden face to the world even when his heart is turning to putty and prides himself on this control over his features and over his words: "I am damn good at not speaking" (p. 347). And so on.

But if there is about Tietjens' principles an element that is merely conventional, that reflects the *noblesse oblige* and pride of the scion of a landed family, there is another element that is most unconventional. His older brother Mark questions Christopher about what has happened to the legacy from his mother, which has in fact trickled away—or poured away—through "loans" to Macmaster and others. Mark objects: "I suppose you don't give money to every fellow that asks for it?" The answer is as succinct as it is unexpected:

> "I do. It's a matter of principle."
>
> "It's lucky," Mark said, "that a lot of fellows don't know that. You wouldn't have much brass left for long."
>
> "I didn't have it for long," Tietjens said. (p. 215)

His forgiveness of his wife is equally unexpected, at least by her. Sylvia at moments regards her husband as deeply immoral, for she believes that she has used him badly and is baffled and humiliated by his apparent willingness to forgive her when she cannot forgive herself. But it is worse than Tietjens' perpetually forgiving her: he finds nothing to forgive. Believing herself pregnant and needing to give her child a name, Sylvia had not only the right but a duty to trepan some man into marrying her. So Tietjens believes. It is equally her right to go on hating all men and incidentally to seek to punish both her husband and lovers. Enmity here seems to him proper as part of the eternal war of the sexes, but this war may be fought, as he believes it has been fought by the two of them, honorably: "I don't care. I can't help it. Those are—those *should* be—the conditions of life amongst decent people. When our next war comes I hope it will be fought out under those conditions. Let us, for God's sake, talk of the gallant enemy. . . . It's the same with you and me" (p. 174). Consequently he must not think of divorcing Sylvia now. They are too old enemies for that.

A man holding principles of this sort will get himself considerably misunderstood, the world being what it is, and as it tries to understand him this world—a "crumbling world"—will progressively give itself away. This is a good strategy, largely because it is a beautifully simple strategy, for Ford to follow. But beautifully simple is what Ford really is not; and as we look harder at Tietjens he shifts and we begin to find him almost as puzzling as his contemporaries found him—which may be a judgment in turn on us and *our* world. I have in mind the first volume's teasing title, *Some Do Not,* and Tietjens' mild but consistent refusal—not to divorce Sylvia, for we understand that, but to take Valentine as his mistress when it is clear that he wants her and equally clear that she is willing to have him. Why do they hold back for nearly ten years?

In the preceding chapter we touched upon this question, but there is more that needs to be said. What is at stake is not, as with divorce, a matter of principle, for Christopher's principles do not preclude a mistress: "Of course, if a man who's a man wants to have a woman, he has her" (p. 18). And when he sees Valentine at the Duchemins—it is only the second time he's seen her—he thinks: "By Jove. . . . What a jolly little mistress she'd make!" (p. 88) Valentine regards herself as the New Woman, sexually liberated, with nothing apparently to restrain her, and by the end of the weekend she is in love. Some do not—but, then, why don't they?

Each of the novels of the trilogy has a title that is played with and tested so that its various facets catch the light; it is turned upside down, stared at, tapped, held up to the ear, examined, and ultimately proved by all that makes up the novel. In the first novel "some do not" appears three times—or four, if we include an additional glancing reference—at widely spaced intervals. The moral meaning of the affair depends on its latent ambiguity, for at least the title does not make quite clear whether "some" is to be thought of as referring to Valentine and Tietjens or to the others. "Some do not" may mean "some refrain from doing" or again it may mean "some fail in their duty." Does the title express praise or blame? When first spoken by one of the characters, the phrase in fact implies neither; it is neutral, no more than a formula for privilege. So Tietjens swings aboard an already moving train (as we have noted) and gets away with it since he is Tietjens of Groby:

"Truly," Macmaster quoted to himself:

> " 'The gods to each ascribe a differing lot:
> Some enter at the portal. Some do not!' " (p. 22)

In its second appearance it takes on the connotations of blame. When, in the early morning accident that follows their all-night buggy ride, their horse is badly bloodied, Christopher administers first aid and stays by the animal, sending Valentine on to rouse a veterinarian. This prompts the following comment:

> The fly-driver touched his age-green hat with his whip.
> "Aye," he said thickly, putting a sovereign into his waistcoat pocket. "Always the gentleman . . . a merciful man is merciful also to his beast. . . . But I wouldn't leave my little wooden 'ut, nor miss my breakfast, for no beast. . . . Some do and some . . . do not." (p. 144)

It is only near the end of the volume that the phrase is applied directly to the question of whether Valentine and Tietjens should or should not be lovers. On the eve of his going out to France for the second time Tietjens' morale weakens; whatever it is that has made him hold back for five years gives way before the temptation to have at the very least a last fling. But, even then, a part of his will refrains, for when he asks Valentine he speaks with an unaccustomed, joyless clumsiness. He blurts out: "Will you be my mistress to-night? I am going out to-morrow at 8:30 from Waterloo" (p. 279). Valentine accepts, but her acceptance is scarcely more eloquent:

> She had answered:
> "Yes! Be at such and such a studio just before twelve. . . . I have to see my brother home. . . . He will be drunk. . . ." She meant to say: "Oh, my darling, I have wanted you so much. . . ." (p. 280)

It is then that an old tramp whose presence Ford does not otherwise account for and who never reappears, but who is just there like an unexplained figure in a fairy tale, makes his memorable comment:

> She went away, up a cockle-shelled path, between ankle-high railings, crying bitterly. An old tramp, with red weeping eyes and a thin white beard, regarded her curiously from where he lay on the grass. He imagined himself the monarch of that landscape.
> "That's women!" he said with the apparently imbecile enigmaticality of the old and the hardened. "Some do!" He spat into the grass; he said: "Ah!" then added: "Some do not!" (p. 280)

And late that night the two agree that their interchange of the afternoon was a mistake: Christopher speaks for them both when he says, "We're the sort that . . . *do not*!" (p. 283)

Which leaves us about where we were—but not quite. Various sorts of refusal have tended to coalesce. The key to Valentine's and Christopher's is not a principle or even an idea but something so old-fashioned in the way of a disposition or attitude that it comes as a slight shock for us to find it in a novel written in the nineteen-twenties: chastity. "There's something beautiful, there's something thrilling about chastity," one of the characters remarks. "Isn't the real symbol Atalanta running fast and not turning aside for the golden apple? That always seemed to me the real truth hidden in the beautiful old legend" (p. 85).

At a time when Aldous Huxley was writing satirically about "chastity belts" and when on the western side of the Atlantic the word had become nearly obsolete (if not what it stood for), Ford managed to take chastity seriously—or perhaps not quite seriously either, since

Valentine replies to these effusions: "You mean like an egg and spoon race?" Nevertheless, Ford managed to make chastity seem attractive, for the "real truth" about Christopher and Valentine is that they must be included among the chaste. It is *pudeur* not principle that keeps them for so long apart.

The very novelty of the conception charms; in some ways Christopher and Valentine are very simple, very innocent: something of the sort is perhaps needed as the pivot for this huge turning (and crumbling) world. It is like the child in Proust, the child that is never quite buried under all the corruption and that we find as surely in Charlus as in Marcel. Quite early Tietjens says to Macmaster, "I stand for monogamy and chastity. And for no talking about it" (p. 18). It seems he really does. "You stand," Tietjens adds, "for lachrymose polygamy." Though Ford can scarcely be credited with having made chastity fashionable again, his making it seem attractive, even if briefly, is a sufficient display of legerdemain and sets him apart from most of the other novelists of the period. Ford himself is scarcely simple or innocent: he accomplishes this feat by shifting the focus of attention from morality to language and back again while we are not looking.

One of Ford Madox Ford's most curious and little-known books is his *Mister Bosphorus and the Muses*, described on the title page as *A Short History of/ Poetry in Britain/ Variety Entertainment/ in Four Acts/ Words by/ Ford Madox Ford/ Music by/ Several Popular Composers/ with Harlequinade, Transformation/ Scene, Cinematograph Effects, and/ Many Other Novelties, as Well as/ Old and Tried Favourites*." It was from *Mister Bosphorus* that Macmaster quoted, anachronistically and inaccurately, when he introduced the title-phrase "some do not." The couplet originally ran:

> The Gods to each ascribe a differing lot!
> Some rest on snowy bosoms! Some do not![6]

Mister Bosphorus and the Muses was published in 1923, a year before the first of the Tietjens books, and between the two there are certain affinities. It is written partly in prose, partly in verse. The action, to

[6] Ford Madox Ford, *Mister Bosphorus and the Muses* (1923), p. 57.

the extent that there is an action, consists of the desertion of the impoverished poet Bosphorus by his Northern Muse, who is staunchly English nineteenth-century, followed by his incarceration in the workhouse and eventual rescue by the Southern Muse—Bosphorus' equivalent for Madame Sélysette or Valentine Wannop—his one true love, European, classical, meridional. The style of Bosphorus' verse alters as the influence of his muses waxes and wanes. The writing calls to mind the famous parodies in *Ulysses*, for, like Joyce, Ford implies there is a connection between word and act, between the prevailing style of a period and its moral insights.

In his mock-classic couplets Ford burlesques the style of the English eighteenth century, whose sensuality (at least in verse) seems almost to burlesque itself and so scarcely offends against chastity—though it may against high seriousness. But it is not Ambrose Philips or Edward Young that Ford is chiefly gunning for in his depiction of the Northern Muse but writers of a century later whose language, even when they are trying to be most moral, often seems softly and sickly suggestive. Ford once wrote:

> The very last thing that these, the last of the Romanticists, desired was precision. On one page of one of Mr. Ruskin's books I have counted the epithet "golden" six times. There are "golden days," "golden-mouthed," "distant golden spire," "golden peaks," and "golden sunset," all of them describing one picture by Turner in which the nearest approach to gold discernible by a precise eye is a mixture of orange-red and madder-brown.[7]

Ruskin and his admired contemporaries are the chief butt in *Mister Bosphorus*, and it is also his presence in *Some Do Not* that permeates the Duchemins' drawing room and sets chastity in a strange light:

> "I don't know," Miss Wannop said, "when I read what Ruskin says about it in the *Crown of Wild Olive*. Or no! It's the *Queen of the Air*. That's his Greek rubbish, isn't it? I always think it seems like an egg-race in which the young woman didn't keep her eyes in the boat. But I suppose it comes to the same thing."
>
> Mrs. Duchemin said:
>
> "My *dear*! Not a word against John Ruskin in *this* house!" (p. 85)

[7] Ford Madox Hueffer, *Memories and Impressions* (1911), p. 65.

Expressed in Ruskin's words in a hothouse atmosphere of the lesser Pre-Raphaelites—what Tietjens calls "a fair blaze of bosoms and nipples and lips and pomegranates"—chastity necessarily becomes somewhat unchaste. As the mad Mr. Duchemin ("the most Ruskin-like of them all") says, licking his thin lips: " 'Chaste!' he shouted. 'Chaste you observe! What a world of suggestion in the word . . .' " (p. 99).

In *Some Do Not* a French concern for the precise word enters not only into Ford's narration but also into the rendering of the thoughts of the characters: we are not allowed to forget that men and women will see often only what their words permit them to see.

> Macmaster quoted to himself:
>
> " 'I looked and saw your eyes in the shadow of your hair. . . .' "
>
> There was no doubt that Mrs. Duchemin's eyes, which were of a dark, pebble blue, were actually in the shadow of her blue-black, very regularly waved hair. (p. 53)

It is then that Macmaster falls in love with Mrs. Duchemin. What he cannot see is her vulgarity, for there is perhaps little in the rhetoric of Rossetti's verse or Ruskin's prose to enable him to see vulgarity. If, on the contrary, his mind had been formed on, say, Heine or on the English naturalist Gilbert White, Macmaster's perceptions would necessarily have been different, and perhaps clearer. It is exactly these writers, together with Ovid and Catullus and, strangely, the anonymous poets who wrote the north-country ballads, who permit Christopher and Valentine to see one another: writers not prudish or mawkish but in their words exact—and in that sense chaste. So:

> "Die Sommer Nacht hat mirs angethan
> Das war en schweigsame Reiten . . ."
>
> he said aloud.
>
> How could you translate that? You couldn't translate it: no one could translate Heine:
>
> "It was the summer night came over me:
> That was silent riding . . ." (p. 128)

Or, from a somewhat different range:

> "He's the last English writer [Gilbert White] that could write," said Tietjens.

"He calls the downs 'those majestic and amusing mountains'," she said. "Where do you get your dreadful Latin pronunciation from? . . ."

"It's '*sublime* and amusing mountains,' not 'majestic and amusing'," Tietjens said. "I got my Latin pronunciation, like all public schoolboys of to-day, from the German."

She answered:

"You would!" (pp. 130–131)

Valentine and Christopher are protected by the conjunction of the sublime and the amusing. Having minds free of the rhetoric of "lachrymose polygamy," they are kept chaste through the very words they use.

Tietjens' tribulations increase as prewar England crumbles around him. The worst constructions are placed on his generous acts: it is variously rumored that Valentine is his mistress and that he has been keeping her on his wife's money, that he is in fact the lover of Edith Ethel Duchemin (later the wife of his best friend), that he has got poor Valentine with child, that he has got Edith Ethel with child, that he is a Socialist, that he is deranged, that he is a religious fanatic, and so on. Through the offices of a banker who does not like him his checks bounce. Tietjens has in general a bad time. In other circumstances all this might seem to be the projection of a paranoid mind, but we believe in Tietjens' tribulations for the most part since we have been made to believe in the crumbling world: at such times, in such places, society must have its scapegoats. "It is, in fact, asking for trouble if you are more altruist than the society that surrounds you" (p. 207).

Ford has gained his desired perspective. In the earlier war novel, *The Marsden Case*, the tribulations of the two central characters were of so obsessive a nature, and were so agonized over by them, that the War remained merely a shadow in the background. In contrast, Tietjens' composure under stress both before and after the outbreak of hostilities makes of him an ideal central observer—a quality that Valentine shares with him. What both observe is not a vast conspiracy but a vast insensitivity, for the impression that comes through strongly—even well into the War—is that this is a crumbling world that has not yet realized it is crumbling. Society is actuated by a curious blend of hysteria and sheer lack of imagination; Tietjens reacts with a blend of outward calm and muffled distress.

Though Ford wisely refrained from depicting the outbreak of war, the events of the fatal day of August 4, 1914, Part One concludes appropriately with the sequence in which General Campion's car, out of control, looms out of the mist and bears down upon Christopher and Valentine—an image that is followed by the bloody shoulder of the horse and shortly afterwards by the General himself in full regalia with row after row of medals, yet somehow shrunk to a tiny comic figure ("a scarlet and white cockatoo") posturing before a bleeding reality that is beyond his, or anyone's, control. These taken together form what Ezra Pound might call an "ideogram" or Eliot the "objective correlative" for the shock that was felt when war broke suddenly on a moderately peaceful and poorly prepared world. All this is implied. But despite the initial shock, Ford leaves the impression that for many of London's citizens the prewar world was slow to die. In Part Two of *Some Do Not* the War is still remote from the awareness of many, and much of English life is outwardly little changed. Mark Tietjens' horse racing continues, as do Edith Ethel Macmaster's Fridays (her salon), though there is now a sprinkling of uniforms among the thinning ranks of her young geniuses.

But the tone of society is already beginning to alter. Civilians find themselves ill at ease in the presence of the army men. As Sylvia puts it, "All the men who aren't hate all the men that are" (p. 161). It is a feeling that appears to be reciprocated; we are told of a bank president (a peer at that) who affected Tietjens "with some of the slight nausea that in those days you felt at contact with the civilian who knew none of your thoughts, phrases or preoccupations" (p. 181). The civilians themselves have suffered change; Tietjens thinks the men who make up the personnel of the government offices are no longer what they once were—"simple honest fellows. Stupid, but relatively disinterested" (p. 236). They have lost some of their honesty and disinterest. Throughout society, beneath a surface callousness runs a suppressed hysteria that breaks out in occasional moments of nearly insane violence: burnings in effigy (this happens to Mrs.

Wannop because her radical son is believed to be "pro-German"), fierce arguments within the family, together with more drinking and a general perceptible coarsening.

Eventually Christopher and Valentine must change too in their apparently fixed relations. The mutual renunciation at the end of *Some Do Not* is the last such renunciation they will make. It is not, as it would be in a novel by Henry James, final. The typical novel by James moves toward an act of rejection—whether of the Baron de Mauves by Mme. de Mauves, of Kate Croy by Morton Densher, or of the spoils of Poynton by Fleda Vetch. Implicit in the personal rejection is a rejection of certain, usually materialistic, tendencies of the society. In this rejection James shares: it is his as well as the characters'. Some of Fords' earlier novels follow him very closely in this respect; for example *The Good Soldier*, where Edward ends by packing Nancy off to India and taking his own life. *Some Do Not* shares in this family resemblance if it is read simply by itself and not as the first of a trilogy. Indeed, if James had been writing *Parade's End* it is hard to think how he would have continued the story. But the end of *Some Do Not* is merely the beginning for Ford.

Tietjens is not merely judge of his society, as Henry James's rejecters are, for even in his rejection he is still deeply implicated in its values. He is (if I may borrow from Howard Nemerov) like a man interpreting a dream while still dreaming the dream, and hence necessarily subject to error. Though Ford has made chastity seem attractive, there nevertheless attaches to Christopher's and Valentine's parting scene—or scenes—a faint aura of absurdity. The old tramp lying in the grass, who "imagined himself the monarch of that landscape," has a further wisdom, and I think Ford knew this. I am reminded of another and more famous old tramp come home after ten years of war, and ten of wandering, with the painful benefit of changed perspectives. Something of the sort must happen to Tietjens too, a consideration which brings us now to the later volumes.

2. *No More Parades*

Bloody and gross though war is, it has its own version of chastity which goes by the familiar name of "parade." As Ford uses it the word "parade" does not mean quite what it would to an American writer, for in addition to denoting a ceremonial public march with banners and band music, in the English army "parade" denotes a muster of troops for inspection and so, by extension, any moment of official duty. ("Do you mind my asking," Tietjens asks at one point, "Are we still on parade? Is this a strafe from General Campion as to the way I command my unit?" [p. 328]) Yet in the present novel the word comes to suggest much more: it implies not merely discipline but good manners, even amenities, ceremony, perhaps—at rare moments —ritual.

> "At the beginning of the war," Tietjens said, "I had to look in on the War Office, and in a room I found a fellow . . . What do you think he was doing . . . What the hell do you think he was doing? He was devising the ceremonial for the disbanding of a Kitchener battalion. You can't say we were not prepared in one matter at least. . . . Well, the end of the show was to be: the adjutant would stand the battalion at ease: the band would play *Land of Hope and Glory*, and then the adjutant would say: *There will be no more parades*. . . . Don't you see how symbolical it was: the band playing *Land of Hope and Glory*, and then the adjutant saying *There will be no more parades?* . . . For there won't. There won't, there damn well won't. . . . No more Hope, no more Glory, no more parades for you and me any more. Nor for the country . . . Nor for the world, I dare say . . . None . . . Gone . . . Na poo, finny! No . . . more . . . parades!" (pp. 306–307)

Parade has helped to make the War possible, and yet the War is destroying parade, as wars always do. This time, however, the destruction threatens to be permanent.

Both halves of this proposition are suggested by the novel's action, as when into a darkened hut in France O Nine Morgan struts, come to deliver his bizarre announcement: " 'Ere's another bloomin' casualty'."Here the stiffness of parade both holds off (for an instant) and *is* the stiffness of death. The whole depot is pre-eminently a place of parade. It is a world of movement orders and counterorders: we see troops being sent toward the front, then called back, then late at night being marched into lines of tents by the light of the moon. But this depot is also a place where parade is perpetually being threatened, where morale is perpetually being broken down, for nothing works here quite as it should. A replacement depot in a war theater is different from a combat unit, and the morale of its men is especially subject to erosion by three things: 1) red tape and regulations, 2) enemy bombing, and 3) memories of women and home. The last is not always the least painful.

Of the soldiers that we see in the hut, Captain Tietjens, Captain McKechnie, and Private Morgan all have wives who appear to have betrayed them. Each has suffered and is suffering. Two of these women are mercifully far away; not, however, Tietjens' Sylvia, who soon enters the scene to set the entire camp at odds and put all parade in jeopardy.

Sylvia has arrived in France unexpectedly (and illegally) in the company of Major Perowne, her former lover; Tietjens learns of her presence shortly after the death of O Nine Morgan. Hers is a hostile presence: the parading soldiers appear to Sylvia to be no more than ridiculous schoolboys; she hates them and hates Christopher for being one of them. Sylvia intends what amounts to the rape of her husband, a second seduction to repeat their original meeting on a train, but with this difference: then she cared next to nothing about Christopher while now her feeling for him amounts to a passion. She means mischief. Husband and wife meet the following day at a French hotel near the camp, have dinner, and retire afterwards to Sylvia's bedroom. Without Tietjens' knowledge the door is left unlocked, and late that evening an elderly drunken general of M.P.'s bursts in, with Sylvia in negligee. Tietjens ejects the general forcefully. Here military decorum reaches its nadir. He is immediately placed under arrest; but the next morning he is released by General Campion, and the novel ends with a comic recovery of parade, its *reductio ad absurdum* in fact: a Commanding General's inspection of a cookhouse.

Such a summary of course does not do justice to the texture of *No More Parades* as a rendering, or to the subtlety of its attitudes toward parade, which are mixed, much like the feelings about chastity in *Some Do Not*, of which they seem to be an outgrowth.

Let us see first what can be said in parade's favor. Parade may be thought of as the principle that produces form; it is the principle also of good form, of coolness, poise, style. It is a function of parade to harmonize and order and so control the madness—the old chaos—that threatens most men at one time or another in this world. It was parade that Macmaster in *Some Do Not* invoked when by his tone ("the snappy intonation of a reproving don") he quelled, if only temporarily, the Reverend Mr. Duchemin's breakfast ravings. In a more literal sense it is parade that in the present book Tietjens invokes in dealing with the disturbed Captain McKechnie—and not McKechnie alone. "There are madmen whose momentarily subconscious selves will respond to a military command as if it were magic. Tietjens remembered having barked 'About . . . turn,' to a poor little lunatic fellow in some camp at home and the fellow who had been galloping hotfoot past his tent, waving a naked bayonet with his pursuers fifty yards behind, had stopped dead and faced about with a military stamp like a guardsman" (p. 298).

The pathos of this anecdote—and pathos there is—derives from the parade shown when the "poor little lunatic fellow" faced about with the military stamp of a guardsman—not just any soldier but one of the king's own. At about this point the ceremonial, even sacramental, implications of parade begin to be felt. It is because Tietjens regards himself as responsible for these as well as for the more obviously disciplinary ranges that his role as commander of a battalion in the giant replacement depot has also its quasi-priestly side.

> Intense dejection, endless muddles, endless follies, endless villainies . . . All these men toys, all these agonies mere occasions for picturesque phrases to be put into politicians' speeches without heart or even intelligence. Hundreds of thousands of men tossed here and there in that sordid and gigantic mud-brownness of midwinter . . . by God, exactly as if they were nuts wilfully picked up and thrown over the shoulder by magpies. . . . But men. Not just populations. Men you worried over there. Each man a man with a backbone, knees, breeches, braces, a rifle, a home, passions, fornications, drunks, pals, some scheme of the universe, corns, inherited diseases, a green-grocer's business, a milk walk, a paper stall, brats, a slut of a wife. . . . The Men: the Other Ranks! And the poor———little officers. God help them. Vice-Chancellor's Latin Prize men. (pp. 296–297)

It is to this welter of suffering men that Tietjens feels obliged to give something, even if his gift is no more than bringing, in the middle of the night, a countermanded draft back into its quarters smartly. In the circumstances he must improvise commands that are not in the book. We find him standing in pyjamas and greatcoat, while the troops march past:

"The draft will move to the left in fours. . . . Form fours . . . Left . . ." Whilst the voices of the sergeants in charge of companies yelped varyingly to a distance in the quick march order he said to himself:

"Extraordinarily glad . . . A strong passion . . . How damn well these fellows move! . . . Cannon fodder . . . Cannon fodder . . . That's what their steps say. . . ." His whole body shook in the grip of the cold that beneath his loose overcoat gnawed his pyjamaed limbs. He could not leave the men, but cantered beside them with the sergeant-major till he came to the head of the column in the open in time to wheel the first double company into a line of ghosts that were tents, silent and austere in the moon's very shadowy light. . . . It appeared to him a magic spectacle. He said to the sergeant-major: "Move the second company to B line, and so on," and stood at the side of the men as they wheeled, stamping, like a wall in motion. He thrust his stick half-way down between the second and third files. "Now then, a four and half a four to the right; remaining half-four and next four to the left. Fall out into first tents to right and left. . . ." He continued saying, "First four and half, this four to the right. . . . Damn you, by the left! How can you tell which beastly four you belong to if you don't march by the left. . . . Remember you're soldiers, not new-chum lumbermen. . . ."

It was sheer exhilaration to freeze there on the downside in the extraordinarily pure air with the extraordinarily fine men. They came round, marking time with the stamp of guardsmen. He said, with tears in his voice:

"Damn it all, I gave them that extra bit of smartness. . . . Damn it all, there's something I've done. . . ." Getting cattle into condition for the slaughterhouse. . . . They were as eager as bullocks running down by Camden Town to Smithfield Market. . . . Seventy per cent of them would never come back. . . . But it's better to go to heaven with your skin shining and master of your limbs than as a hulking lout. . . . The Almighty's orderly room will welcome you better in all probability. . . . He continued exclaiming monotonously: "Remaining half-four and next four to the left. . . . Hold your beastly tongues when you fall out. I can't hear myself give orders. . . ." It lasted a long time. Then they were all swallowed up. (pp. 361–362)

There is no way to quote less of this passage and still suggest its effect. The fate of the men is implied in the last sentence, but to be swallowed up is not quite the same as to be blotted out. In Ford's trilogy this is the crowning instance of parade, for here, despite Tietjens' being dressed somewhat inappropriately in pyjamas and his "cantering" beside the men, the absurdity of the situation is no more than latent. Here parade comes as close as it ever can to being sacrament. This scene occurs near the end of Part One of *No More Parades.* Sylvia has not yet appeared in person, though her presence is already beginning to be felt and with it a spirit that is critical of these (or any) martial pieties. We are not to scorn her view. Indeed, a good deal can be said against parade—and must be said—by anyone who looks at the matter dispassionately.

Tietjens himself had been critical enough earlier. In *Some Do Not* we were told: "Army officers seemed to him pathetic. They spluttered and roared: to make men jump smartly: at the end of apoplectic efforts the men jumped smartly. But there was the end of it" (p. 127). The really telling point against parade—as against ritual, magic spells, manners and decorum, and perhaps form of all sorts—is its ridiculous, almost impertinent inadequacy when it is opposed to the lawless chaos of forces (the "undisciplined squads of emotion") with which by its nature it has to contend. Parade at last cannot control these, since it remains in part at least a function of the forces it seeks to control—like the "church militant" in a fallen world. Drills, which are pretty in peacetime, in war are implicated in the whole senseless mess.

In Ford's particular dialectic, parade's antithesis is madness, and there is much madness in *Parade's End.* The theater of war is no less than "an ocean of mental suffering" in which Christopher Tietjens plays his part and, like the others, must be immersed. On his earlier tour at the front he was the victim of shell shock and total amnesia; here in *No More Parades* he alternately worries about impending madness and accepts it with a hard indifference. Ford wrote—as I have mentioned more than once—of the days following the Armistice, "You may say that every one who had taken physical part in the war was then mad. No one could have come through that shattering experience and still view life and mankind with any normal vision."[8] His aeshetic problem was to find the means of doing justice both to the madness and to the coming-through. In the preceding chapter we

[8] *It Was the Nightingale,* p. 63.

considered one such means: to project war as a "blurred fairy tale" culminating, as even blurred fairy tales must, in a "happy ending." But madness is also susceptible of being treated more directly.

It may be that at this level he is less successful, revealing less knowledge of madness than of magic (like other writers one can think of). The conditions of success are limiting. To treat war as a collective madness requires of the novelist a nice feeling for the disputed borderline between the mad and the sane and also an ability to see the mad as growing out of the sane—as being nourished by the sane—much as war is nourished by peace, since each war defines the peace that precedes it. To treat members of a particular generation as collectively mad is to regard madness less as an aberration than as the continuum in which all live, almost as the air they breathe. Of course, if we come to feel that it is simply the author whose brain is blurred, we may doubt the relevance of what his brain registers, just as if we feel that he is totally untouched—totally sane—we will probably shrug off his vision. What then of our author, of whom H. G. Wells wrote, "The pre-war F. M. H. was tortuous but understandable, the post-war F. M. H. was incurably *crazy*"?[9] How is it with him?

On the whole, Ford's madmen in *Parade's End* are plausible enough, though at first it is a little surprising how many of them there are. These include: the Reverend Mr. Duchemin; Macmaster's Cambridge friend, Sim, who "on society occasions would stand up and shout or sit down and whisper the most unthinkable indecencies"; Macmaster's nephew McKechnie; Lord Port Scatho's brother-in-law; and the anonymous "little lunatic fellow" that Tietjens had stopped in his tracks by shouting "About turn!" In addition to these psychotics or near-psychotics we are shown Mrs. Wannop with her tendency to "drift," who after her husband's death was "out of her mind for grief" and who for three days after the outbreak of war was again "clean out of her mind." There is her "unbalanced" and obnoxious son, who drinks too much and who reveals, as Tietjens can see, what some later writer might call "unmistakable schizoid tendencies":

> When they had caught him up he had been haranguing under black hanging trees, with an Oxford voice, an immobile policeman. . . .

[9] See Douglas Goldring, *Trained for Genius* (1949), p. 90.

Tietjens himself he had always addressed with the voice and accent of a common seaman; with his coarsened surface voice!

He had the two personalities. (p. 282)

There is also Sylvia's mother—an aging philanthropist too fond of hothouse flowers—who confesses: "I tell you I've walked behind a man's back and nearly screamed because of the desire to put my nails into the veins of his neck. It was a fascination" (p. 27). There is Tietjens' own "mad-scene." What is his name? he wonders:

"I lay and worried and worried, and thought how discreditable it would appear if a nurse came along and asked me and I didn't know. . . . Then a lot of people carried pieces of a nurse down the hut: the Germans' bombs had done that of course. They were still dropping about the place. . . .

"The poor dear wasn't dead. . . . I wish she had been. Her name was Beatrice Carmichael . . . the first name I learned after my collapse. She's dead now of course. . . . That seemed to wake up a fellow on the other side of the room with a lot of blood coming through the bandages on his head. . . . He rolled out of his bed and, without a word, walked across the hut and began to strangle me. . . .

"He let out a number of ear-piercing shrieks and lots of orderlies came and pulled him off me and sat all over him. Then he began to shout '*Faith*!' He shouted: 'Faith! . . . Faith! . . . Faith! . . .' at intervals of two seconds, as far as I could tell by my pulse, until four in the morning, when he died. . . . I don't know whether it was a religious exhortation or a woman's name, but I disliked him a good deal because he started my tortures, such as they were." (pp. 169–170)

Tietjens' tortures were apparently partly modeled on Ford's own. In his biography Goldring quotes from a letter written by Ford while he was a patient in France: "All day I am as stupid as an owl and all night I lie awake and perceive the ward to be full of Huns of forbidding aspect."[10] Ford had suffered a breakdown at least once before. He writes whimsically of this earlier illness in *Return to Yesterday*. "From 1903 to 1906 illness removed me from most activities. The illness was purely imaginary; that made it none the better. It was enhanced by wickedly unskillful doctoring." He describes having wandered "from nerve-cure to nerve-cure" in England and on the

[10] *Ibid.*, pp. 194–195.

Continent, "mostly in Germany." His trouble was diagnosed as "agoraphobia and intense depression." Therapy was disagreeable, including "cold water baths and tepid soda-water douches." His diet was restricted at one sanatorium to "pork and iced cream" and at another to "dried peas and grapes."

The director of the *Kaltwasser-Heilanstalt* was an immense, thin man with a long grey waterfall of beard through which he passed his fingers, as if cautiously, before he ever made a remark. He usually wore black spectacles. In the effort to prove that my troubles had an obscure sexual origin, he would suddenly produce from his desk and flash before my eyes indecent photographs of a singular banality. He expected me to throw fits or to faint. I didn't.[11]

Whenever mental doctors appear in the pages of Ford's books they are figures of fun (with the sole exception of the witchlike Katya Lascarides in *A Call*). In *Mister Bosphorus and the Muses* we eavesdrop on two demonic children who are doing a little homework to surprise their analyst:

"Let's get back to Freud.
Good Doctor Wilkinson is due to-morrow
To ask about our dreams. We'll startle him
About the golden cup!" (p. 33)

In his other postwar books the name of Freud is increasingly heard. Sylvia rather modishly, and with bravado, in *Some Do Not* says about a certain Mrs. Profumo and the black masses that she has been attending: "Does it shock you? . . . I'll admit it was a bit thick. . . . But I've done with it. I prefer to pin my faith to Mrs. Vanderdecken [a medium?]. And, of course, Freud" (p. 37). In her set there is much talk of the new psychology. Someone at a party is overheard saying something about "inhibition" and even Father Consett uses the word "complexes." But how much do any of them really know? One imagines probably not much.

There is considerable evidence, however, that in *Parade's End* Ford was himself drawing on more than a smattering of Freudian lore and putting it to good use. (This may partly account for Osbert

[11] See Ford Madox Ford, *Return to Yesterday* (1932), p. 261 ff.

Sitwell's snide, clever coinage "Freud Madox Fraud.") As a writer Ford had been concerned for a long time with shock, and as a man he seems to have been particularly subject to jolts of various sorts; consequently we might expect him to reveal an interest in the theory of trauma, as when he has Valentine say, "You cannot suffer a great sexual shock and ever be the same. Or not for years" (p. 231). There are other instances of Freudian accretions upon a Fordian base. Ford's method of impressionist "rendering" had always presupposed the existence of some subconscious, or unconscious, or semiconscious state. He wrote in the 1914 essay "On Impressionism":

If to-day, at lunch at your club, you heard an irascible member making a long speech about the fish, what you remember will not be his exact words. . . . You will remember this gentleman's starting eyes, his grunts between words, that he was fond of saying 'damnable, damnable, damnable.' You will remember that the man at the same table with you was talking about morals, and that your boots were too tight, whilst you were trying, in *your under mind*, to arrange a meeting with some lady.[12]

But in his postwar writing for the first time there is question of a theory of the unconscious. For example:

The sudden entrance of Macmaster gave . . . [Tietjens] a really terrible physical shock. He nearly vomited: his brain reeled and the room fell about. He drank a great quantity of whisky in front of Macmaster's goggling eyes; but even at that he couldn't talk, and he dropped into his bed faintly aware of his friend's efforts to loosen his clothes. He had, he knew, carried the suppression of thought in his conscious mind so far that his unconscious self had taken command and had, for the time, paralysed both his body and his mind. (pp. 79–80)

Since Ford probably made no very clear distinction between suppression and repression (he seems to use the words interchangeably), what he says later of Captain McKechnie both relates to the above passage and takes in by implication their whole society: "The repressions of the passionate drive them mad" (p. 296). Already in *Some Do Not* we were shown the would-be angelic Mr. Duchemin who had tried to put into practice John Ruskin's kind of chastity:

[12] Ford Madox Hueffer, "On Impressionism," *Poetry and Drama*, 1 (June, 1914), 174–175. The italics are mine.

He shouted three obscene words and went on in his Oxford Movement voice: "But chastity . . ."

"When my revered preceptor . . . drove away in the carriage on his wedding day he said to his bride: 'We will live like the blessed angels!' How sublime! I, too, after my nuptials . . ."

Mrs. Duchemin suddenly screamed:

"Oh . . . *no*!" (p. 99)

Admittedly, Valentine's and Christopher's chastity is of a different sort, but as the theme of madness spreads through *No More Parades* (like Tietjens' memory of the stain of O Nine Morgan's blood) it becomes increasingly difficult for either the reader or the principal characters to place much reliance in chastity, military parade, reticence, or even self-control: some more affirmative basis of value will be needed by those who survive Armageddon than the rather priggish "some do not."

Captain McKechnie is a thematic character: he largely embodies the madness and pathetic senselessness of war while reminding us that such madness is not all of war's making. When Tietjens first observes him he wonders: "There were a great many kinds of madness. What kind was this? The fellow was not drunk. He talked like a drunkard, but he was not drunk" (pp. 297–298). McKechnie is still, at this time, mad only in spells: he can remain in possession of himself so long as the noise of bombing and antiaircraft does not grow too intense. Only then does he give way to irrational fear (not that there isn't much to be rationally afraid of).

His problem really was: could he stand the——noise that would probably accompany their [the planes'] return? He had to get really into his head that this was an open space to all intents and purposes. There would not be splinters of stone flying about. He was ready to be hit by iron, steel, lead, copper, or brass shell rims, but not by beastly splinters of stone knocked off house fronts. (p. 305)

And why is that? His fear, though it is expressed in battle, appears to derive from McKechnie's relations with his wife, the stone fragments coming to symbolize their splintered marriage:

That consideration had come to him during his beastly, his beastly, his infernal, damnable leave in London, when just such a filthy row had been going on. . . . Divorce leave! . . . The memory seemed to burst inside him with the noise of one of those beastly enormous tin-pot crashes—and it always came when guns made that particular kind of tin-pot crash: the two came together, the internal one and the crash outside. He felt that chimney-pots were going to crash on his head. (p. 305)

In *No More Parades* McKechnie, the dully mad, has replaced his dully sane uncle Vincent Macmaster as Tietjens' opposite and alter ego. Both Tietjens and McKechnie are captains, both are university men, and both suffer from their wives. Where Tietjens has chronic difficulties with his godfather (General Campion), McKechnie's are with his uncle. Tietjens writes sonnets to relieve his feelings, while the other can turn them into Latin hexameters—and does. One is mad, the other fears madness. So long as hostilities continue McKechnie sticks like a bur. He is not only present during the three hideous and funny days of *No More Parades* but he is present again in *A Man Could Stand Up*, airing his grievances, mumbling about sonnets and uncles, and making Tietjens' hard life at the front harder still. Tietjens is not free of him until he is free of the war; that is, until Armistice Day, when McKechnie at last has to be committed.

But if McKechnie establishes, and carries, one of the novel's principal themes, he does not set its tone, for, despite the sense of a world gone mad, gloom is not the prevailing mood of *No More Parades* nor what we tend to remember afterwards. Ford's fiction may be about the end of something—sometimes, indeed, it seems to be about the end of everything—but in its crispness and jauntiness it is instinct with parade.

Upon reflection, this depiction of war seems more than anything comic, though we will probably have to stretch our conception of comedy and we may have to scrap some received ideas about what subjects are intrinsically funny. Bedroom farce, for example, is usually regarded as comic, dying not. And yet . . . Consider Sylvia. Eros and Thanatos, Venus bedded with Mars; who is Sylvia and what is she? Though a pacifist who hates war, Sylvia has a curious affinity with it. It is fitting, I think, that where Valentine Wannop is unimaginable in wartime France, Ford should bring Sylvia across the Channel and develop her line of destruction in counterpoint with that of the war. She herself seems half to realize that they are one flesh, one perverse will, when she perceives (as she puts it) that she is "in the very belly of the ugly affair" (p. 438). In her, peace and war meet cruelly and absurdly. Sylvia dominates *No More Parades* from the moment when, shortly after O Nine Morgan's death, Tietjens has a premonition of her presence: "It was as if an immense cat were parading, fascinated and fatal, round that hut" (p. 315). "Parading" is indeed the *mot juste*.

In many ways Sylvia stands for the Ruling Classes and the established order of prewar England, the order which led to and then collapsed in the War. Though she gives little thought to it, she is its direct embodiment. She is, throughout, a wonderfully convincing depiction of tradition in decay, not the quiet decay of paralysis and torpor but the decay of boredom, of keeping up appearances, which in her case leads to endless restless irresponsibility. She is cruel, yet brave and noble, even at moments generous—not wholly distinct from Tietjens himself. That is one reason why Sylvia is so convincing. All of these characters are members of the same leisured society, which Ford once summarized as "fairly unavailing, materialist, emasculated—and doomed."[13] Sylvia is merely its more virulent, and in some ways most attractive, manifestation. Tietjens breaks with it only in his final break with her.

In the trilogy Sylvia appears to be increasingly out of control. As far back as the beginning of *Some Do Not* Father Consett had prophesied "her hell on earth will come when her husband goes running, blind, head down, mad after another woman" (p. 42). Tietjens has not quite done that, but his continued holding back, his mooning along with Valentine just barely on the horizon, perhaps has goaded Sylvia even more. More and more the gay escapades—her "pulling the strings of shower-baths"—together with the elaborate lies she has erected on her husband's tottering reputation, take on some of the stridency of desperation. Sylvia's most recent prank, to attach herself to Major Perowne and blithely, without papers, to make her way to France (where she complains to the General that her husband has taken some of her sheets), represents a kind of crisis. For, oddly,

[13] *Return to Yesterday*, p. 210.

Sylvia too is one of the chaste—"She was, and had been for many years, absolutely continent" (p. 150)—although we are told that she knew her set "had to have, above their assemblies as it were, a light vapour of the airs and habits of the brothel." For five years now she has not slept with her husband nor, apparently, with other men, and during that time she has fallen in love with him, passionately if sadistically. At last she is determined to bring him to heel. But France is not quite what Sylvia imagined it to be, and under the pressure of insane noise during still another air raid her repressions break out in something that is close to madness:

> There occurred to her irreverent mind a sentence of one of the Duchess of Marlborough's letters to Queen Anne. The duchess had visited the general during one of his campaigns in Flanders. "My Lord," she wrote, "did me the honour three times in his boots!" . . . The sort of thing she would remember . . .
>
> But the tumult increased to an incredible volume: even the thrillings of the near-by gramophone of two hundred horse-power, or whatever it was, became mere shimmerings of a gold thread in the drab fabric of sound. She screamed blasphemies that she was hardly aware of knowing. She had to scream against the noise; she was no more responsible for the blasphemy than if she had lost her identity under an anesthetic. She *had* lost her identity. . . . She was one of this crowd! (pp. 439–440)

This brings Sylvia fully into the ambit of war. But by far the most important point about Sylvia, and one which might easily be overlooked, is that she possesses, among her other attributes, those of a splendid comic heroine—or comic villainess rather: the embarrassments that Sylvia creates are nearly always funny and the humor is not lost on her. She has wit and a nice sense of the incongruous, sometimes at her own expense as when (in *The Last Post*) she finally gives up Tietjens to poor Valentine, who by then is his *de facto* wife, saying:

> "An the King will have my head I carena what he may do with my . . ." (p. 826)

The allusion is to the words of her fellow papist Fraser of Lovat just before he was executed in the 'Forty-five. Ford explains:

> They had told him on the scaffold that if he would make some sort of submission to George II they would spare his body from being exhibited in

quarters on the spikes of the buildings in Edinburgh. And Fraser had answered: "An the King will have my heid I care not what he may do with my—," naming a part of a gentleman that is not now mentioned in drawing rooms. (p. 755)

Sylvia, indeed, comes close to being Ford's muse, since his characteristic juxtapositions, "perspectives by incongruity" where war is superimposed on peace and peace on war, create a way of looking at things that can probably be described only as comic. Comedy permeates Ford's world at even its grimmest, as in the death of O Nine Morgan: in our last glimpse of him (in person, as distinct from the recalls) he is being carried "in a bandy chair out of the hut. His arms over his shoulders waved a jocular farewell" (p. 311).

Northrop Frye has observed that comedy

> contains a potential tragedy within itself. With regard to the latter, Aristophanes is full of traces of the original death of the hero which preceded his resurrection in the ritual. Even in New Comedy the dramatist usually tries to bring his action as close to a tragic overthrow of the hero as he can get it, and reverses this movement as suddenly as possible.[14]

The ritual elements of death and resurrection might be looked for here, especially in such a novel as *A Man Could Stand Up*, for Christopher Tietjens has about him something of the aura of the sacrificial hero. As Sylvia remarks to Sergeant-Major Cowley, "They used to say: 'He saved others; himself he could not save' " (p. 404). This is, however, not the path that I wish to follow at present. Rather, I would like to revert to certain consequences of the curiously closed-in quality of Ford's scene.

Out there and a little beyond is unnamed horror: the horror of what lies beyond the front lines, of No Man's Land, the Unknown, from which for the most part we take cover with varying degrees of success. Were the action placed out there, as it is in much of the *Iliad*, it would necessarily be tragic. But Ford's characters remain enclosed, boxed-up, holed-in. We—the readers and the characters—await the inevitable intrusion, and when it comes it is horrid and macabre, but not

[14] Northrop Frye, "The Argument of Comedy," *English Institute Essays 1948*, ed. D. A. Robertson, Jr. (New York: Columbia University Press, 1949), p. 65.

tragic. It is more than anything else absurd, since in this shut-in scene the social norms of a life of reason and common sense, or what passes for them—in particular such matters as rank and class—despite all have been preserved. These are quite simply incommensurate with the intruding horror, and it with them. So when death enters Tietjens' hut in the guise of O Nine Morgan, for a brief time the social norms are shattered—for one thing, blood gets on an officer's shoes—but the normal is quickly re-established. Perhaps it is this very quickness that keeps the rhythm comic.

The recurrences of this pattern suggest a further structural principle: each such boxed-in interior—whether of hut, or hotel bedroom, or elegantly appointed railway carriage, or dugout at the front—comes to suggest all the rest. As the novel proceeds, we are translated as though by metamorphosis from one interior to the next (often in violation of chronological sequence), and to the extent that we take notice of this strange transmogrifying process—this sliding-away of panels—we will probably find it comic. Indeed, these rapidly shifting perspectives are implicit in the minutiae of Ford's style, and as such they make themselves felt from the start.

The shadings of Ford's war comedy cover a wide range; some of these queer juxtapositions, though they make their point, seem fairly obvious. There is Tietjens composing the sonnet in less than three minutes to rhymes supplied by McKechnie, while signing incredible numbers of papers for the soldiers of a draft that is on its way up the line. There is the highly efficient Sergeant-Major Cowley's penchant for sudden transformations: "The sergeant-major, now a deferential shopwalker in a lady's store, pointed out that they had had urgent instructions not to send up the draft . . ." (p. 324); "the sergeant-major, now a very important solicitor's most confidential clerk, etc." (p. 326). There is the inappropriate name of the General's war horse, "Sweedlepumpkins." But at its best the comedy is not obvious at all, as in this glimpse of Sylvia's peculiar way of torturing her husband: "She warned him that, if he got killed, she should cut down the great cedar at the south-west corner of Groby. It kept all the light out of the principal drawing-room and the bed-rooms above it. . . . He winced: he certainly winced at that" (p. 430). There are also bits of battle humor which are so intimately a part of the atmosphere of an army at—or near—the front: "Do you know the only time the King must salute a private soldier and the private takes no notice? . . . When 'e's dead" (p. 433). From this, Ford modulates to something far more eerie, as the Sergeant-Major explains to Mrs. Tietjens how at Noircourt the Captain had stumbled:

> "Caught 'is foot, 'e 'ad, between two 'ands. . . . Sticking up out of the frozen ground . . . As it might be in prayer. . . . Like this!" He elevated his two hands, the cigar between the fingers, the wrists close together and the fingers slightly curled inwards: "Sticking up in the moonlight. . . . Poor devil!" (p. 434)

Horrible? Haunting? Funny? Or terrifying? It is hard to say which this is. It is all and more, with its faint echoes of Dante's ninth circle; and it is not quite like any other writing about war that one can think of, nor like any other twentieth-century prose. It is a high and horrible comedy where much compassion is played off against the unrelenting pressure of the absurd.

The whole movement of the trilogy comes to a brief rest, as it should, in a fine scene at the end of *No More Parades,* a repetition of the familiar pattern of intrusion—if we can so characterize a general's inspection. The fall of France at this point appears imminent, and the fall of Tietjens with it; yet the ending Ford supplies is comic, light, and gay. It follows the disagreeable private interview between General Campion and Tietjens and serves both as a recapitulation and a comic coda. Tietjens, we are told, had earlier been given a moment to alert his cookhouse of the approaching inspection.

> "You can do what you please," the sergeant-cook said, "but there will always be one piece of clothing in a locker for a G.O.C.I.C.'s inspection. And the general always walks straight up to that locker and has it opened. I've seen General Campion do it three times."
>
> "If there's any found this time, the man it belongs to goes for a D.C.M.," Tietjens said. "See that there's a clean diet-sheet on the messing board."
>
> "The generals really like to find dirty clothing," the sergeant-cook said; "it gives them something to talk about if they don't know anything else about cook-houses. . . . I'll put up my own diet-sheet, sir. . . . I suppose you can keep the general back for twenty minutes or so? It's all I ask." (p. 449)

At the conclusion of his interview with Tietjens the General said:

"... You can fall out."

Tietjens said:

"My cook-houses, sir ... Sergeant-Cook Case will be very disappointed. ... He told me that you couldn't find anything wrong if I gave him ten minutes to prepare. ..."

The general said:

"Case ... Case ... Case was in the drums when we were at Delhi. He ought to be at least Quartermaster by now. ... But he had a woman he called his sister ..."

Tietjens said:

"He still sends money to his sister."

The general said:

"He went absent over her when he was colour-sergeant and was reduced to the ranks. ... Twenty years ago that must be! ... Yes, I'll see your dinners!" (p. 499)

Sergeant Case's situation, it is readily apparent, is analogous to Tietjens', but with a difference—he is a man who has been both ruined and not ruined by his woman. He keys us for the novel's finale. *No More Parades* began with the words "When you came in"; it ends with a locker door opening.

The building paused, as when a godhead descends. In breathless focusing of eyes the godhead, frail and shining, walked with short steps up to a high-priest who had a walrus moustache and, with seven medals on his Sunday tunic, gazed away into eternity. The general tapped the sergeant's Good Conduct ribbon with the heel of his crop. All stretched ears heard him say:

"How's your sister, Case? ..."

Gazing away, the sergeant said:

"I'm thinking of making her Mrs. Case ..."

Slightly leaving him, in the direction of high, varnished, pitch-pine panels, the general said:

"I'll recommend you for a Quartermaster's commission any day you wish. ... Do you remember Sir Garnet inspecting field kitchens at Quetta?"

All the white tubular beings with global eyes resembled the pierrots of a child's Christmas nightmare. The general said: "Stand at ease, men ...

Stand easy!" They moved as white objects move in a childish dream. It was all childish. Their eyes rolled.

Sergeant Case gazed away into infinite distance.

"My sister would not like it, sir," he said. "I'm better off as a first-class warrant officer!"

With his light step the shining general went swiftly to the varnished panels in the eastern aisle of the cathedral. The white figure beside them became instantly tubular, motionless and global-eyed. On the panels were painted: TEA! SUGAR! SALT! CURRY PDR! FLOUR! PEPPER!

The general tapped with the heel of his crop on the locker-panel labelled PEPPER: the top, right-hand locker-panel. He said to the tubular, global-eyed white figure beside it: "Open that, will you, my man? . . ."

To Tietjens this was like the sudden bursting out of the regimental quick-step, as after a funeral with military honours the band and drums march away, back to barracks. (p. 500)

3. *A Man Could Stand Up*

In some ways the last volume of the trilogy is the most beautifully constructed of the Tietjens books: here more than anywhere else form is determined by the principle of balancing the petty details against the great outlines. Ford takes us at last into the trenches, toward which the whole action has been driving, but our stay is brief and the central episode is presented almost casually, as if it were an interlude. *A Man Could Stand Up* begins and ends with Valentine on Armistice Day, but in between its beginning and its ending is a flashback to a morning at the front several months earlier, where we encounter Tietjens, temporarily in command of a reduced battalion, anxiously awaiting an enemy attack. We see him all told for hardly more than an hour, yet in that time much happens. During the enemy's preliminary bombardment Tietjens is blown up by a freak detonation and buried deep in mud—but curiously he is not hurt and he manages to acquit himself with coolness throughout. He receives, nevertheless, a curt reprimand when an inspecting general (Campion once again) appears unexpectedly, with eyes only for his soiled uniform. Ford then returns us to Armistice Day afternoon and evening, and the novel ends happily but rather wildly with Christopher and Valentine united at last, though in an empty house and surrounded (invaded, in fact) by a rejoicing populace that is nearly delirious with relief.

In so constructing *A Man Could Stand Up,* Ford achieves a kind of "sonata" whose specifications (as suggested in an earlier chapter) would be: ". . . first subject: Hero. Second subject: Heroine. . . . And then Working Out and Recapitulation." The order of Hero and Heroine is here reversed, but otherwise that would be a fair description of this novel's form. The first subject and the second subject—here peace and war—are not so much opposed as juxtaposed, for, however it may be in a true sonata, in a novel by Ford the basic elements are not allowed to suggest a simple contrast. Rather it is a matter of "ordinariness set against ordinariness in a slightly different plane" (as in a Braque still life). Normally the plane of peace and the plane of war would be regarded as more than slightly different, yet Ford's eye is sharpest for resemblances between his two subjects, for unexpected concurrences between Tietjens' morning in the trenches and Valentine's morning in an English schoolhouse.

For example, in both episodes the scene is cloistered, strictly confined: to deep trenches in the one and to an enclosed schoolyard in the other. Both hero and heroine are only temporarily "in command"; Tietjens' colonel is sick, alcoholic, and *hors de combat,* while Valentine's head mistress has turned over the girls to her in her capacity as gym instructress to keep them doing "jerks" until after the peace has been officially announced. Both feel themselves amateurs in these roles and somewhat out of place. Both episodes involve waiting—for the H-hour of a German attack and for eleven o'clock of that magic morning of November 11, 1918. In examining both their mornings Ford manages to create the impression that it is all in a day's work and yet that this particular day is crucial.

A Man Could Stand Up is also formally interesting in reflecting a further stage in Ford's peculiar responsiveness to time. With each new novel of the trilogy a shorter period elapses between beginning and ending: *Some Do Not* opens in the summer of 1912 and closes in 1917; *No More Parades* opens apparently during the winter of 1917 and closes two days later; *A Man Could Stand Up* begins and ends on Armistice Day. (And, continuing this progression, in *The Last Post* the whole will be limited to approximately one hour.) It is as though from novel to novel elapsed time were shrinking and subjective time (Bergson's *durée*) were expanding. We note that the characters are increasingly tied down; they become less active and more ruminative: in their lives there is an added confinement and an incipient liberation.

Time hangs especially heavy in Part Two, the long sequence in the trenches where Ford orchestrates the various worries, recollections, and slowdowns and speedups of time that comprise Christopher Tietjens' awareness during approximately an hour's apprehensive waiting for the expected enemy attack in force. The sequence opens with the sun not yet risen. Tietjens, temporarily in command of a reduced battalion, is first discovered looking over the parapet at mists that "mopped and mowed, fantastically," obliterating the enemy lines. Through his mind pass memories of the attack of two nights before, in which the Germans had come over in gas masks, looking "like goblin pigs with sore eyes." The sequence divides into two halves. The first hundred-odd pages are a minute-by-minute account of three bad quarters of an hour of standing by for the enemy artillery strafe to begin. It is as though Time itself were pinned down. The section ends with the opening of the bombardment and with Tietjens' being summoned to the dugout of the battalion commander, the sick colonel whom he is about to relieve. The second section follows Tietjens' emergence from the H.Q. dugout and culminates wierdly in his being blown up. A huge shell designed to destroy trench parapets digs deep into the mud under him, goes off and lifts Tietjens gently into the air. Time slows still more. When he comes down again, he is buried in the mud yet astonishingly is not hurt. This scene is a turning point; time, having had a stop, resumes its more normal movement.

Time in the meanwhile has entered Ford's war scene in other ways. An important part of any combat soldier's mind is his sense of futurity, his premonitions of who will be killed and (perhaps less often) who will not. Such premonitions can be misleading, and not all of Tietjens' are fulfilled. In the case of the aging lieutenant in charge of *A* Company who lives in the desperate hope of seeing his children again Tietjens intuits, correctly as it turns out, that he will not see them. About himself, Tietjens is sure he will not be killed but instead will be wounded, and he thinks he knows the exact spot: the soft bit of flesh just above the right collarbone. But this time he is wrong; he is not wounded, though before going home again he will be both gassed and shell-shocked.

Tietjens is also beset by the fantasy that if by a kind of magic levitation he were able to float a few feet above the flooring of the trench and remain suspended at a level with a certain splash of whitewash shaped like a cockscomb he would be perfectly safe. In fact he has his mind still on the cockscomb while he is being blown up:

> He was looking at Aranjuez from a considerable height. He was enjoying a considerable view. Aranjuez's face had a rapt expression—like that of a man composing poetry. Long dollops of liquid mud surrounded them in the air. Like black pancakes being tossed. He thought: ". . . We are being blown up!" The earth turned like a weary hippopotamus. It settled down slowly over the face of Lance-Corporal Duckett who lay on his side, and went on in a slow wave.
>
> It was slow, slow, slow . . . like a slowed down movie. The earth manoeuvred for an infinite time. He remained suspended in space. As if he were suspended as he had wanted to be in front of that cockscomb in whitewash. Coincidence!
>
> The earth sucked slowly and composedly at his feet.
>
> It assimilated his calves, his thighs. It imprisoned him above the waist. His arms being free, he resembled a man in a life-buoy. The earth moved him slowly. It was solidish. (p. 637)

This passage depends throughout on "ordinariness set against ordinariness in a slightly different plane." It is Ford at his most characteristic and best. A new experience is built up out of several old ones, the strangeness of the new experience being its very familiarity —as in those queer moments called *déjà vu* when a house, a bit of broken wall, or a curve of road insist that we have been here before, though we know we never could have been. Ford brings together the familiar experience of enjoying a considerable view; the somewhat less familiar experience of watching a person composing poetry; the pleasant domestic sight of pancakes (black pancakes) being tossed; the delightful but rather disturbing experience of being rolled about in heavy surf (though here there are sinister overtones of shipwreck, with Tietjens resembling "a man in a life-buoy," and perhaps echoes from the beaching scene in Stephen Crane's "The Open Boat" where the Correspondent is tossed through the air over the capsized boat while he disinterestedly watches the other men tumbling in the waves around him). Different planes of reality intersect in Tietjens' long moment, even the mild contemplation of a spectator at the zoo—though the weary hippo is Time itself. The passage is laden with time ("an infinite time") and in that respect it is the whole book (and all of Ford's books) in miniature.

Ford once explained that what the impressionist wanted to express in his prose were those "queer effects of real life that are like so many views seen through bright glass—through glass so bright that whilst you perceive through it a landscape or a backyard, you are aware that on its surface it reflects a face of a person behind you."[15] Where in some of his early—and also his very late—novels he seems to have strained after such effects, the war called them naturally into being. The words needed to have very clean edges to make them possible; the prose had to be "French" to that extent. In this connection let me introduce one additional exhibit, a rendering of H-hour, in its own small way as mysterious as the instant of death—or Eliot's moment in the rose garden.

We are told that the German strafe will begin in one minute, and what are Tietjens' subalterns doing? We find them talking about sonnets, Tietjens, as a trick, having once written a sonnet in two and a half minutes. They shake their heads over that. Tietjens, however, has his mind on other things: he is musing on the time needed for the Allies to throw in massive reserves, probably a matter of months. Ford places the three incommensurable intervals side by side without comment, creating a juxtaposition of some nicety:

> But it would take time. Months! Anything like adequate reinforcements would take months. . . .
>
> In one minute the German barrage was due.
>
> Aranjuez said:
>
> "You can write a sonnet in two and a half minutes, sir . . ." (pp. 597–598)

The minute comes to an end and is punctuated by means of a further

[15] "On Impressionism," *Poetry and Drama,* I, 174.

juxtaposition—of the tiny and the very large, the near and the distant, two different kinds of briefness:

> It was due now. The second-hand of Tietjens watch, like an animated pointer of hair, kicked a little on the stroke of the minute. . . . "Crumb!" said the punctual, distant sound. (p. 599)

A Man Could Stand Up derives its title from a brief conversation between Tietjens and one of his sergeants as they crouch in a gravelly trench that has been dug into the side of a hill. The sergeant says "Then a man could stand hup on an ill. . . . You really mean to say, sir, that you think a man will be able to stand up on a bleedin' ill" (p. 570). Tietjens has largely been making talk, for the future is still a matter more of phatic than vatic concern. Yet this seems to be a turning point; his half-conscious thoughts swing toward what he is going to do *après la guerre finit,* and an image appears to him suddenly of the green English countryside, George Herbert's country, with himself, surprisingly, as a quiet country parson, Greek testament clutched under his arm, standing upright and alone on a small hill.

This is only an image—a velleity, not a decision; Tietjens lacks, for one thing, George Herbert's faith. But he knows that he possesses the heart of Valentine Wannop and he resolves here at last to take her heart and body—without sanction of either church or state. So there will be no country parsonage for him. It is, none the less, a turning point.

He knows now that he is going to stand up—one way if not another —not alone, but with Valentine. The phrase "a man could stand up" seems phallic if one chooses to see it so. It suggests both resurrection from the underworld of the trenches and Christopher's passional renewal after a decade not so much of chastity as of complete continence: a new life and, as for women, his first (excepting only the wild train ride with Sylvia, which was followed by nothing). As with the other volumes, the title here is functional; it seems almost to generate two remarkable images: one comic, of someone's standing up on a hill *at the front*—the extreme case of Ford's hard trench humor—and the other a foretaste of Valentine and, for Tietjens, of paradise.

It would probably be best to consider the comic stance first, since it represents all that Tietjens most wants to leave behind. Ford's comic sense does not desert him as we have moved forward. Trench humor can be appreciated only in—or near—the trenches; but it can be conjured up for disinterested contemplation by the novelist, not for laughs (heaven forbid!), rather for its strangeness—like the strangeness of a "blurred fairy tale." So Ford introduces us to the one man who does stand up on a hill in plain view of the enemy, only to become the great clown of the front lines:

> A gunner had been looking through his glasses. He had said to Tietjens: "Look at that fat. . . .!" And through the glasses lent him, Tietjens had seen, on a hillside in the direction of Martinpuich, a fat Hun, in shirt and trousers, carrying in his right hand a food tin from which he was feeding himself with his left. A fat, lousy object: suggesting an angler on a quiet day. The gunner had said to Tietjens:
>
> "Keep your glass on him!"
>
> And they had chased that miserable German about that naked hillside, with shells, for ten minutes. Whichever way he bolted, they put a shell in front of him. Then they let him go. His action, when he had realised that they were really attending to him, had been exactly that of a rabbit dodging out of the wheat the reapers have just reached. At last he just lay down. He wasn't killed. They had seen him get up and walk off later. Still carrying his bait can!
>
> His antics had afforded those gunners infinite amusement. . . . Irresponsible people, gunners! (pp. 586–587)

Granted.

The other instance is of another fat man, Tietjens himself. It is an analogous situation, but as it were in a different key. There is perhaps comedy in their juxtaposition. We are told, "A mound existed between Tietjens and B Company trench, considerably higher than you could see over. A vast mound; a miniature Primrose Hill" (p. 626). That mound is the setting for Tietjens' scene. To be sure, he does not quite stand up on the top of it—he is no clown—but by luxuriously reclining on its reverse slope, as he does, he has a little oasis of peaceful hillside on which to meditate on his girl and his future—a brief respite before the attack. In place of the Hun's "bait can" Tietjens has laid before him an elegant repast.

The Corporal balanced himself before Tietjens on the slope of the mound. He blushed, rubbing his right sole on his left instep, holding in his right hand a small tin can and a cup, in his left an immaculate towel containing a small cube. . . . He set the coffee tin, cup and towel on a flat stone that stuck out of that heap; the towel unfolded, served as a table-cloth; there appeared three heaps of ethereal sandwiches. (pp. 631–632)

Tietjens muses—complacently—that from the point of view of his club's peacetime cuisine his present satisfaction may be "gastronomically reprehensible."

But, for the matter of that, fancy drawing deep breaths of satisfaction over the mere fact of lying—in command of a battalion!—on a slope, in the clear air, with twenty thousand—two myriad!—corks making noises overhead and the German guns directing their projectiles so that they were slowly approaching! Fancy! (pp. 633–634)

And then a moment later he is blown up.

The actual blowing-up, which we have already looked at, is crucial. It is the still point about which the whole action of the trilogy turns. Going to war and coming home again is an archetypal, even an epic action, in spite of Ford's playing down the element of heroism. Tietjens' ordeal is thus a kind of hero journey. What is needed at some point in any hero journey is a moment of supernatural descent or ascent—like Odysseus' drop into the underworld or Troilus' (or Dante's) rising into highest heaven—something distinctly difficult to arrange in a novel that, like Ford's, for all its temperamental strangeness, never breaks wholly with the naturalistic convention. The explosion, then, is providential: it makes possible Tietjens' moment of levitation, his near magical Assumption.

When, at the end of Chaucer's poem, Troilus looked down and back, he laughed; for he had gained a new perspective. Tietjens too has been gaining a new perspective—but slowly. The basic conflict between reticence, or "chastity" of thought and feeling, on the one hand, and disruptive madness, on the other, was established early in *Some Do Not*, and in the next volume it was suggested that the victory would go to madness in a world where there would be no more parades (or if not to madness, to a random decay of meaning). In *A Man Could Stand Up* the pattern is not essentially changed, but with the experience of the trenches, culminating in a combination of burial and blow-up, the significance for Tietjens, the "look" of the pattern, has changed—rather like the "magical" advertisement that he once remarked on to Valentine:

"Do you know these soap advertisement signs that read differently from several angles? As you come up to them you read 'Monkey's Soap'; if you look back when you've passed it's 'Needs no Rinsing'." (p. 234)

So for "madness" and "parade," which come to change their values as we the readers—together with Christopher, Valentine, and Sylvia—look back. It is as though the first two volumes, with their growing emphasis upon the absurd had read "Monkey's Soap"; it is only in the third that we realize that out of the absurd something redeeming and pure must come—that, in fact, Monkey's Soap needs no rinsing.

The mythic accident of the blow-up does not so much produce a change of mind in Tietjens as signal it, since the experience of war has gradually been making itself felt. More and more he has been pried loose from his earlier earth-bound avatar as the Yorkshire Tory squire, and by this time Tietjens has become almost dematerialized. If at home the effect of war has been a general coarsening, in the trenches the reverse appears to be true. Even the enemy are spoken of as "ghostly Huns" when they put in a frightening nocturnal appearance:

They had appeared with startling suddenness and as if with a supernatural silence, beneath a din so overwhelming that you could not any longer bother to notice it. They were there, as it were, under a glass dome of silence that sheltered beneath that dark tumult. (p. 551)

That glass dome of silence is war's "magic and invisible tent," and all who enter it will come back changed.

When she first hears of Tietjens' return on Armistice Day morning the image that comes to Valentine's mind is "a grey ball of mist." In *Some Do Not* the lovers had appeared solid enough types even when riding *through* the mist; now Tietjens' substance has changed, it has lightened. Yet it would be wrong to regard this as a loss of substance: it is, rather, a loss of grossness, an etherialization, as is suggested by the almost Eucharistic lunch that we have already remarked on, taken by Tietjens in the still sunlight immediately before he is blown up and served by the youthful Corporal Duckett who, strangely, makes him think of Valentine:

He would never forget the keen, clean flavour of the sandwiches nor the warm generosity of the sweet, be-rummed coffee! In the blue air of that April hill-side. All the objects on that white towel were defined: with iridescent edges. The boy's face, too! Perhaps not physically iridescent. His breath, too, was very easy. Pure air! (p. 632)

At the beginning of the trilogy madness was something at all costs to be avoided; we had a chance to observe Vincent Macmaster's neat handling of the insane Duchemin with coolness and skill—with parade—since madmen must not be allowed to upset the decorum of an English breakfast. It is only considerably later that we entertain the wild surmise that perhaps madness is sometimes less deadly than an English breakfast—that there are times when it would in fact be folly not to be mad. There is something Shakespearean about this. Madness looks in two directions. It is equated both with war's senseless chaos and despair and with the adequate response to these, quite a different thing. As Edgar discovered, there is reason in madness, for it is only madmen who can magically encompass, and so comprehend, a mad world by becoming its destined scapegoats and witnesses. Consequently, Christopher must lose his memory to the extent that he forgets his identity and, later, his brother Mark must be struck dumb by a paralytic stroke—and so suffer silence—before either comes to such knowledge.

To be sure, they are perhaps closer to Edgar than to Lear; yet, though neither is insane, both Christopher and Mark are repeatedly regarded as "mad" by the less understanding among their acquaintance, a harsh judgment that is mitigated somewhat by the few sympathetic souls who make no such mistake and who in their own small way are "mad" too—for example, Valentine when she talks to Lady Macmaster on Armistice Day morning. (Here the telephone with its poor connection is the appropriate medium for such discoveries.)

Valentine with the receiver at her ear was plunged immediately into incomprehensible news uttered by a voice that she seemed half to remember. Right in the middle of a sentence it hit her:

". . . that he ought presumably to be under control, which you mightn't like!"; after that the noise burst out again and rendered the voice inaudible.

It occurred to her that probably at that minute the whole population of the world needed to be under control; she knew she herself did. (p. 503)

"Needed," that is, from the point of view of such as Lady Macmaster —for within a few minutes Valentine joyfully kicks over the traces for good and all. In the head mistress' office, tendering her resignation, she thinks: "No more respect. . . . For the Equator! For the Metric system. For Sir Walter Scott! Or George Washington! Or Abraham Lincoln! Or the Seventh Commandment! ! ! ! ! !" (p. 511)

So it is, also, with Tietjens. Where in *No More Parades* he had appeared to mourn a loss that was beyond his power to prevent, in *A Man Could Stand Up* we find Christopher actively rejecting parade when he rejects for his defining role the persona of the English gentleman. In the trenches the "some do not" theme comes down at last to this ironic reflection: "Gentlemen don't earn money. Gentlemen, as a mater of fact, don't do anything. They exist. Perfuming the air like Madonna lilies" (p. 589). When shortly afterwards he does do something and, following the great explosion, digs Corporal Duckett out of the mud that has encased him, Tietjens realizes with surprise that this is the first time that he has ever had to exert himself to the full: "It was a condemnation of a civilisation that he, Tietjens, possessed of enormous physical strength, should never have needed to use it before" (p. 638).

Of course it would be wrong to exaggerate this change in attitude. Tietjens is still Tietjens and he is certainly not entirely happy that "the feudal spirit" is broken. He reflects that the new world will be in many ways a tiresome place. But, recognizing this, he no longer merely endures the decline of parade passively: he embraces it now with a hard-earned joy.

Tietjens was never going to live at Groby. No more feudal atmosphere! He was going to live, he figured, in a four-room attic-flat, on the top of one of the Inns of Court. With Valentine Wannop. *Because* of Valentine Wannop! . . . He wanted to be alone with Heaven. . . . He drank his last cup of warm, sweetened coffee, laced with rum. . . . He drew a deep breath. (p. 633)

The rejection of parade—Ford's and Tietjens'—is expressed with finality by letting us see another military inspection, Campion's last. This follows immediately on Tietjens' extricating himself and his men from the mud. Where the preceding volume had ended on the note of a godhead descending, the frail and shining general who was so beautifully in rapport with the sergeant-cook and the tubular assistants frozen at attention—the last unchallenged instance of parade—General Campion now stumbles into a wet brown world where any inspection in the circumstances could be only an impertinence. Gone is his quiet voice of command, and all that remains is a flutter of senile outrage. Indeed, the general is no longer for Tietjens a "he" but has dwindled to a manikin, an "it":

Leaning, in the communication trench, against the corrugated iron that boasted a great whitewashed A, in a very clean thin Burberry boasting half a bushel of badges of rank—worsted crowns and things!—and in a small tin hat that looked elegant, was a slight figure. How the *devil* can you make a tin hat look elegant! It carried a hunting switch and wore spurs. An Inspecting General. The General said benevolently:

"Who are you?" and then with irritation: "Where the devil is the officer commanding this Battalion? Why can't he be found?" He added: "You're disgustingly dirty. Like a blackamoor. I suppose you've an explanation."

Tietjens was being spoken to by General Campion. In a hell of a temper. He stood to attention like a scarecrow.

He said:

"I am in command of this Battalion, sir. I am Tietjens, second-in-command. Now in command temporarily. I could not be found because I was buried. Temporarily."

The General said:

"You. . . . Good God!" and fell back a step, his jaw dropping. He said: "I've just come from London!" And then: ". . . They said this was the smartest battalion in my unit!" and snorted with passion. He added: "Neither my galloper nor Levin can find you or get you found. And there you come strolling along with your hands in your pockets!" . . .

He said:

"I've just had a scratch, sir. I was feeling in my pockets for my field-dressing."

The General said:

"A fellow like you has no right to be where he can be wounded. Your place is the lines of communication. I was mad when I sent you here. I shall send you back."

He added:

"You can fall out. I want neither your assistance nor your information. They said there was a damn smart officer in command here. I wanted to see him. . . . Of the name of . . . Of the name of . . . It does not matter. Fall out. . . ." (pp. 642–644)

This passage, like its companion from *No More Parades*, I have quoted at length. Much might be pointed out, but really the General's last broken sentence tells the whole story. No more need be said. Hereafter, Tietjens will have to stand alone and without swank—or alone except for Valentine at his side.

In the final pages of *A Man Could Stand Up* (which have been discussed already in the chapter on fairy tale), as in those other passages we have been considering, is found very nearly the full range of Ford's writing: a French feeling for the exact word, juxtaposition of elements, a vibration between the great outlines and the petty details together with the queer, characteristic humor that results, and a nearly flawless timing. It is, I submit, here rather than in the brilliant but slighter *The Good Soldier* that Ford, if anywhere, put into a novel *all* that he knew about writing.

We have come a long way since we boarded the "perfectly appointed railway carriage" of 1912 whose leather straps "were of virgin newness," and it might be reasonable to suppose that now we have reached some destination. Ford has carried us beyond the edge of silence and then has brought us back again. He has accomplished his original aim of showing "the world as it culminated in war" by permitting us to see it through the eyes of a central observer whose tribulations hold our attention all the while he continues to observe his crumbling world. The movement of the action has been spiral. We have in fact entered ever deeper into the circlings of Tietjens' affair but with the curious consequence that the tighter Ford's beautifully articulated form encloses his material the more the story itself seems gradually to open. It is welcome and appropriate that a story which began with two young men just sitting should end with a now not so young man and a not so very young woman dancing, and with the final, hopeful words: "On an elephant. A dear, meal-sack elephant. She was setting out on. . . ."

vi. TAPS FOR A NOVEL

Then some drunken man on the church steps opposite had begun to play the bugle. Long calls. . . . Continuing for ever.
—*The Last Post*

There is something rather ghostly about *The Last Post,* where various familiar figures crowd about the dying Mark's bedside and neither he nor the reader is quite sure whether they are flesh and blood: they resemble the *revenants* Marie Léonie fears at night. There is even something a little ghostly about Ford's Dedicatory Letter, in which he regrets that he has not been allowed to leave Christopher Tietjens "to rest beneath bowery vines." "Do you not find . . . in the case of certain dead people you cannot feel that they are indeed gone from this world? You can only know it, you can only believe it. . . . So then, for me, it is with Tietjens."[1] This mortuary feeling gets into the writing and, despite a splendid final sequence, it is hard to escape a recurring impression that the lifeblood has gone out of the enterprise.

In a letter suggesting *Parade's End* as the title for an omnibus edition, Ford wrote in 1930: "I strongly wish to omit *Last Post* from the edition. I do not like the book and have never liked it and always intended to end up with *A Man Could Stand Up*."[2] One sympathizes with the author's wishes. Yet *The Last Post* is still with us in the big Knopf edition, and, when all is said, probably rightly so.

[1] Ford Madox Ford, *The Last Post* (1928), vii.
[2] See Douglas Goldring, *Trained for Genius* (1949), p. 258.

It is hard to be certain. The question of where to bring a novel to an end was unanswerable for Ford in theory, since a novel was to be the history of an affair and Ford recognized that "there is in life nothing final. So that even 'affairs' never really have an end as far as the lives of the actors are concerned. . . . For no force is ever lost, and the ripple raised by a stone, striking upon the bank of a pool, goes on communicating its force for ever."[3] How far the novelist traces the ripple is a matter, then, of tact, not fact. Ford believed he should trace it to the moment of maximum implication, the point where an attentive reader would be able to imagine the rest. Does the ending of *A Man Could Stand Up* bring us to that point? Probably not.

If the novel had been Valentine's story, the answer would be different, for by the close of *A Man Could Stand Up* we know all that is essential about her. Valentine is setting out upon an adventure on a "meal-sack elephant," like a child at the circus, and she will go wherever it takes her. And where is that? It will be somewhere underground, since her union with Tietjens must remain illicit. It appears to them both that Sylvia will grant no divorce, and Tietjens is still reluctant to divorce his wife. We know also all that we need of Valentine's reasons for being willing to go along on the adventure (beyond her love for Tietjens). Valentine is the child of her age, a modernist, who as a suffragette is used to outraging public opinion. To live with Tietjens unmarried is not for her, as for Sylvia it would be, a sin. But we need to know much more about him. How is Tietjens to provide for her? More generally, how will he make his peace with postwar England?

Also, with respect to form, it seems wrong to let the novel come to an end in London. *Parade's End* had opened with two young men on their way down to the country, and it should close in the country, in the interest of that circularity that was a major aspect of Ford's New Form. The novelist, he explained once, "to keep his work together, and, as it were, within one frame, repeats at the end the mood, and recalls the episodes of the beginning, of his book."[4] Ford here resembles Mark Tietjens' wife Marie Léonie:

[3] Ford Madox Hueffer, *A Call* (1910), p. 299.

[4] Ford Madox Ford, *The March of Literature: From Confucius' Day to Our Own* (1938), p. 368.

Her conversation had another quality that continually amused . . . [Mark]: she always ended it with the topic with which she had chosen to begin. Thus, today having chosen to begin with *navets de Paris*, with Paris turnips she would end, and it amused him to observe how on each occasion she would bring the topic back. (p. 683)

Amusement seems the right emphasis. Perhaps there is always something a little frivolous about form—be that as it may, it *is* more amusing for the novel to end in the country. It is, I think, right that Marie Léonie, a comic character, should preside over *The Last Post*, for despite the pathos of Mark's death the ending—like the long novel before it—is fundamentally comic. Consider one aspect: It is traditionally in the spirit of comedy to bring everyone on at the end. According to one writer on comedy, Northrop Frye:

As the hero gets closer to the heroine and opposition is overcome, all the right-thinking people come over to his side. Thus a new social unit is formed on the stage, and the moment that this social unit crystallizes is the moment of the comic resolution. In the last scene, when the dramatist usually tries to get all his characters on the stage at once, the audience witnesses the birth of a renewed sense of social integration.[5]

So in *The Last Post*: almost everybody left is brought "on stage," crowded on: Christopher, Sylvia, their son Michael, Edith Ethel Macmaster, General Campion, Ruggles, Valentine, and Marie Léonie; and there are also several newcomers, Gunning, Lord Fittleworth, Mrs. Lowther, Mrs. de Bray Pape, and two or three others. These circulate confusedly about the dying Mark, who in frozen-faced silence manages to maintain to the last his sense of the ridiculous.

Frye's analysis continues:

This new social integration may be called, first, a kind of moral norm and, second, the pattern of a free society. We can see this more clearly if we look at the sort of characters who impede the progress of the comedy toward the hero's victory. These are always people who are in some kind of mental bondage, who are helplessly driven by ruling passions, neurotic

[5] Northrop Frye, "The Argument of Comedy," *English Institute Essays 1948*, ed. D. A. Robertson, Jr. (New York: Columbia University Press, 1949), pp. 60–61.

compulsions, social rituals, and selfishness. The miser, the hypochondriac, the hypocrite, the pedant, the snob: these are humors, people who do not fully know what they are doing, who are slaves to a predictable self-imposed pattern of behavior. What we call the moral norm is, then, not morality but deliverance from moral bondage. (p. 61)

These remarks apply here not only to obvious "humor characters" like Mrs. de Bray Pape (who believes she is the reincarnation of Mme. de Maintenon and behaves accordingly) or Lady Macmaster with her endless grievances, but to Sylvia—obsessed, possessed, bewitched and bewitching—and finally to Tietjens himself.

Tietjens is the hero, but, as the saying goes, he has been his own worst enemy. Earlier in the story he too was bound by "social rituals" and by snobbery. I believe the critics, incidentally, have been far too ready to applaud his various strong stands, such as:

"I stand for monogamy and chastity. And for no talking about it. Of course if a man who's a man wants to have a woman he has her. And again, no talking about it." (p. 18)

Paul Pickrel was among the first to point out the unreasonableness of Tietjens' refusing to divorce his wife on principle, because a gentleman *does not*, while subjecting Valentine Wannop to the ostracism of bearing his child out of wedlock.[6] Well, it was unreasonable, and I see no reason to suppose that Ford was too blind to see that it was. ("State, underline and emphasize the fact how you will it is impossible to get into the heads of even intelligent public critics the fact that the opinions of a novelist's characters as stated in any novel are not of necessity the opinions of the novelist. It cannot be done."[7]) But, as we have seen, Tietjens learns. Falling in love with Valentine was the first stage of his sentimental education; what follows is his progressive liberation, often high comedy, culminating in the cutting-down of the great gloomy cedar tree at Groby, after which we are told the curse will be off the family. At the end even Sylvia is won over,

[6] See Paul Pickrel, "Outstanding Novels," *Yale Review*, XL, 1 (Autumn, 1950), 189–190.

[7] Ford Madox Ford, *No More Parades* (1925), p. v.

promising a divorce, and we are left with the impression that she too has been liberated when she takes upon herself the responsibility of shooing the unredeemed—and unredeemable—Mrs. de Bray Pape off the premises.

The Last Post is needed, then, to show the resurgence that was promised by the title of the preceding volume, *A Man Could Stand Up*. In point of fact, Tietjens could barely stand when on that Armistice Day afternoon Valentine encountered him staggering down the stairs of his house, his eyes bulging, an old cabinet under his arm. Afterwards, it is true, he dances; but that is not enough: in the circumstances, it is too near to being a dance of death. Something more affirmative is needed. Perhaps a birth? What Ford required for his final thematic statement was a birth and a death together.

2

To emphasize too strongly a comic resolution would be misleading, for Ford's ending is subtle; the prevailing sense of loss is nearly as great as the sense of liberation. The loss is England's. More than lives and more even than talent, Ford believed that some conception of what England was, or might still become, had disappeared during the struggle. Here the speechless Mark becomes his mouthpiece. Though Mark has retired from the world and even from articulate speech, he attests more persistently than the others to the sense of loss. He reflects: "On Armistice Day they had played the Last Post on the steps of the church under Marie Léonie's windows. . . . The Last Post! . . . The Last of England!" (p. 727) We are told: "As he saw things public life had become—and must remain for a long period—so demoralized by the members of the then Government with their devious foreign policies and their intimacies with a class of shady financiers . . . that the only remedy was for the real governing classes to retire altogether" (p. 745). Mark sums up the collective enemy as "Scotch grocers, Frankfort financiers, Welsh pettifoggers, Midland armament manufacturers and South Country incompetents"; against them he pits "old standards of North Country commonsense and English probity" (pp. 745–746).

Ford presumably did not agree entirely; for one thing his own ties were with the south of England. Also, the old standards were surely not quite what Mark thought them to be. Mark is as inflexible as his hard bowler hat. He too is in part a humor character, and for that reason he must go; yet Ford shared his sense of loss. So viewed, Christopher's and Valentine's withdrawal from London—their union unsanctioned by church and state—together with Mark's paralysis and speechlessness, takes on a more general meaning. It becomes the embodiment, as Ford saw it, of the "real governing classes' " retirement from public life.

Mark's washing his hands of the whole business is in fact a good deal more than snobbery or North Country prejudice. It is based on the pragmatic moral code of "Do what you want and then take what you get for it"—Ford's own categorical imperative. Mark believed

> it was the worst disservice you could do to your foes not to let them know that remorseless consequences follow determined actions. To interfere in order to show fellows that if they did what they wanted they need not of necessity take what they got for it was in effect to commit a sin against God. If the Germans did not experience that in the sight of the world there was an end of Europe and the world. What was to hinder endless recurrences of what had happened near a place called Gemmenich on the 4th of August, 1914, at six o'clock in the morning? There was nothing to hinder it. (p. 774)

Mark's stroke comes when he learns that the Allies will not pursue the German armies onto their own soil. That for him is the end.

Shortly before the news reached him on Armistice Night he was disturbed on his sickbed by a drunken bugler's playing taps—what the English call "the last post." This phrase, giving the final volume its title, recurs a number of times to be punned on and played with. Mark "could not remember," we are told, "that, after childhood, he had ever had a penny out of Groby. They would not accept the post: they had taken others. . . . Well, this was his, Mark's, last post." And Ford adds: "He could have smiled at his grim joke" (p. 741). There is also the more literal meaning of *post,* in the sense in which Mark is the last post, the last thing upright and anchored. So at least Sylvia finds him when, angry and wishing a confrontation, she wonders:

"What was she given beauty—the dangerous remains of beauty!—for if not to impress it on the unimpressible! She ought to be given the chance at least once more to try her irresistible ram against that immovable post" (p. 806).

Such stiff posts as Mark suggest the largest and most inflexible of all, Groby Great Tree, 160 feet in height, which was said to have been planted at the birth of Great Frandfather Tietjens (though it must be somewhat older than that). The tree has been traditionally connected with the Tietjens' fortunes. Throughout *The Last Post* it is threatened, and at the end we learn that it is down. What is at first surprising is that Mark—though he and Christopher have been warned—remains indifferent to the tree's fate. Or perhaps he would like to see it down, for it is associated with a curse that has been on Groby (according to an old book, *Spelden on Sacrilege*) since the first Tietjens was given the estate "over the head of . . . [Catholic] fellows in Dutch William's time" (p. 755). Mark is no papist sympathizer, but, as we have been told, he would not accept the post. Let what will be, be.

Local folklore had held that the huge tree "did not like the house." In sober fact "its roots tore chunks out of the foundations and two or three times the trunk had had to be bricked into the front wall" (pp. 758–759). Its uprooting at the hands of Mrs. de Bray Pape is thus a final peripety; but, unlike our response to Mark's death or to the expected birth of Valentine's child, we hardly know whether to be glad or sorry. The next owner of Groby will be Catholic, Sylvia's son Michael; the fortunes of the Tietjens seem about to mend. On the other hand, Groby has lost its chief distinction, and the old house has lost its front wall, which collapsed when the tree's roots were extracted. One whole wing is in ruins. The curse has been removed—if it has—at the cost of a radical reduction: Tietjens can never be "Tietjens of Groby" again in the old way. Mark Tietjens' last words (except for the appeal to Valentine, "Hold my hand!") are "Groby Great Tree is down." At the end, death and resurgence, loss and gain—comedy and pathos—remain in delicate balance.

3

Certain details should not be overlooked in testing the balance of the ending. Ford has come a long way from the mood of despair and the sardonic irony of *The Good Soldier* (which is not at all to say that he has written a better book). Nothing makes the difference clearer than certain superficial resemblances. For example, an electric cord. The door to Florence's room, Dowell had told us, "was locked because she was nervous about thieves; but an electric contrivance on a cord was understood to be attached to her little wrist. She had only to press a bulb to raise the house" (p. 89). A similar contrivance connects Mark Tietjens and Marie Léonie: "For the night they had an alarm that was connected by a wire from his bed to hers. Hers was in a room that gave onto the orchard. If he so much as stirred in his bed the bell would ring in her ear" (p. 698). There is a world of difference between the two connections (electric and other) between husband and wife. In the former example the whole situation was false: nothing was wrong with Florence's heart except that she had none; she was not afraid of thieves; the locked door was simply a device to ensure privacy for her intimacies with Edward or Jimmy, or whoever. But for Mark and Marie Léonie the electric bond is the real thing.

Mark's wordless and helpless condition after his stroke recalls Nancy's condition after her collapse, but here the difference is even greater. Nancy's two utterances repeated over and over—"I believe in an Omnipotent Deity" and "shuttlecocks"—cancel out completely. They are more than irony: between them any meaning that might attach to her fate is ground to pieces. These two extremes reappear in Mark's musings, but reconciled and humanized. There is, on the one hand, what Mark regards as perhaps his only claim to fame, a remarkable feat achieved in youth when, shooting near the sea, he brought down at a single shot "two terns, a sandpiper and a herring gull." Later these were stuffed and mounted, "the herring gull stiff on a mossy rock; the sandpiper doing obeisance before it, the terns flying, one on each side." He reflects: "Probably that was the only memorial to him, Mark Tietjens, at Groby" (p. 829). Mark improvises an epitaph: "*Here lies one whose name was writ in sea-birds*" (p. 832). But as it turns out he is not permitted even that memorial; when the front wall of Groby collapses, Mrs. Pape has the case of birds thrown onto the rubble heap. These birds, then, and their queer history are the equivalent of Nancy's "shuttlecocks." At the other extreme is the great night:

> Mark Tietjens had lain considering the satisfaction of a great night he had lately passed. Or perhaps not lately: at some time.
>
> Lying out there in the black nights the sky seemed enormous. You could understand how somewhere heaven could be concealed in it. And tranquil at times. Then you felt the earth wheeling through infinity. (p. 828)

The two extremes are opposed but not hopelessly opposed; and if his prevailing mood is ironic, it is not nihilistic.

So too, though Mark's final words in dialect have about them a suggestion of nonsense—as he speaks painfully with his tongue filling his mouth—what he says is not nonsense. It is his expression of love. Mark has suffered silence and found a language commensurate with it; but it is not the language of this world.

By the end of *The Last Post* he is no longer the humor character he had appeared to be earlier—at least not at the very end. The uprooting of Groby Great Tree coincides with Mark's *re*-rooting, his reversion to an older type. Through suffering he has changed from the umbrella-carrying public official, with his perfectly regulated life, his Stilton, lamb chops and buttered toast, a mistress to be visited on certain days of the week and favorite race tracks to be visited on certain (not necessarily other) days—from all this to a silent North Countryman deeply rooted in the land. It is a little surprising that the change does not strike us as more surprising, or that Mark does not come to seem an altogether different person. Probably the hard Yorkshireman had been there all along, hidden under the siftings of custom, and Ford is less presenting character development than a discovery, or uncovering. By the end Mark can accept with equanimity the uprooting of Groby Great Tree, for his own roots go even deeper.

The change is suggested by the changed quality of his speech. Through the long novel we have been led from the idiom of the scarcely dead—or not quite dead—Pre-Raphaelites at the beginning of *Some Do Not* (Vincent Macmaster's "so circumspect and right") gradually back into the eighteenth century (Sylvia's "My Lord did me the honour three times in his boots") and thence into the seventeenth. Something of the sort we have noted already. We are told that Mark "accepted Christopher's dictum that he himself was an eighteenth century bloke and was only forestalled when he had wanted to tell Christopher that he was more old-fashioned still—a sort of seventeenth century Anglican who ought to be strolling in a grove with Greek Testament beneath the arm and all" (p. 762). Yet as we overhear his thoughts in *The Last Post,* Mark too is more seventeenth- than eighteenth-century. His pastoral-agrarian surroundings, the seventeenth-century cottage and old Gunning have doubtless something to do with it. Mark's equivocal silence finds expression in the familiar *From henceforth he never would speak word.* Thoughts of the silent Iago evoke these thoughts of his creator: "Good man, Shakespeare! All-round man in a way, too. Probably very like Gunning. Knew Queen Elizabeth's habits when hunting; also very likely how to hedge, thatch, break up a deer or a hare or a hog, and how to serve a writ and write bad French" (p. 679). But when, painfully, Mark speaks aloud again, his speech is older even than the seventeenth century.

It goes back to what Hugh Kenner in writing about Ford has called "faery England,"[8] the England that existed before the Elizabethans and their "preposterous drum-beating" and whose passing Richard Corbet lamented three centuries ago in "The Fairies' Farewell." It is an England that at the time Ford was writing was still marginally alive in the dialect and mentality of someone like Gunning, the Tietjens' handy man. "Gunnings had been in the course of years, painted blue, a Druid-worshipper, later, a Duke Robert of Normandy, illiterately burning towns and begetting bastards—and eventually—actually at the moment—a man of all works, half-full of fidelity, half blatant, hairy" (pp. 814–815). Mark comes to resemble Gunning, if not in the begetting of bastards then in his imperturbability. He recalls with pleasure the story of the Yorkshireman on the top of Mount Ararat who, with his chin just out of water when Noah came sailing up, said: "It's boon to tak oop." (It's bound to clear up.) But in some ways the dying Mark is closer to the past than even Gunning is. The dialect that he speaks at the end leads back to the childhood of England and to his own childhood, the time of the sea-birds and before.

[8] Hugh Kenner, "Remember That I have Remembered," *Gnomon* (New York: McDowell Obolensky, 1958), p. 160.

He said:

"Did ye ever hear tell o' t' Yorkshireman. . . . On Mount Ara . . . Ara . . ."

He had not spoken for so long. His tongue appeared to fill his mouth; his mouth to be twisted to one side. It was growing dark. He said:

"Put your ear close to my mouth . . ." She cried out!

He whispered:

" *'Twas the mid o' the night and the barnies grat*
And the mither beneath the mauld heard that."

. . . "An old song. My nurse sang it. . . . Never thou let thy barnie weep for thy sharp tongue to thy goodman. . . . A good man! . . . Groby Great Tree is down. . . ."

He said: "Hold my hand!"

She inserted her hand beneath the sheet and his hot hand closed on hers. Then it relaxed. (pp. 835–836)

4

Backed as they are by the hundreds of pages that go before, the last twenty of *Parade's End* are the most moving Ford ever wrote. They testify to the supreme value of preparing effects. Yet as a whole *The Last Post* is weaker than its companion volumes. The scene of Mark's death is more than the end of the Tietjens saga, it is the end of Ford as a great novelist. He never wrote anything remotely like it again.

Loss of vigor is reflected throughout in the characters, many of whom seem to have lost their grip—especially Christopher. During the first three volumes he managed to keep his face properly wooden no matter what was happening. In *The Last Post*—where he scarcely appears in person but is seen from the points of view of others —Tietjens often winces, goggles with his eyes while searching for words, and in the end makes off like a dejected bulldog. We learn to our surprise that the weak expression "for God's sake" is typical of him. He has grown forgetful and inefficient: he loses prints, permits himself to be cheated by his business partner, and is unable to prevent Groby's destruction. Most of the parade seems to have gone out of him. As for his sense of humor, it has vanished, and gone is his old air of phlegm and command. So too for Valentine. In the earlier volumes she made it a point of honor to preserve a certain pawkiness while worrying M.P.'s on the golf course, correcting Tietjen's Latin, or keeping muscular girls doing jerks on Armistice Day. Here she cowers behind locked doors. And General Campion, who in France was almost Godlike in his shining uniform, is now just and old "pantaloon" to be made to whimper by Sylvia.

Now none of these changes is exactly out of character. They might be accounted for by the strain of war or the anticlimax of the Armistice; yet it is hard to escape the impression that they reflect Ford's own fatigue. There are also pages of considerable tediousness. The retrospections (always a characteristic of Ford's style) become almost intolerable. In the earlier volumes they served the double function of reminding the reader of what had gone before and of expressing the inner life—the life of memory—of the characters. They were more than offset by new events. It is only in *The Last Post* that they are nearly everything.

Weakest of all, perhaps, are the new characters, particularly Marie Léonie and Mrs. de Bray Pape, a stereotyped Frenchwoman and the caricature of an American. They are both bores. Mrs. Pape looks to the future; it is, as Ford puts it, "an American day." Ford's Americans—with the possible exception of John and Florence Dowell and Florence's two maiden aunts—are always abysmal. Unlike some European writers (Nabokov comes to mind), he had almost no ear for American speech, yet seems to have prided himself that he had. (He makes Mrs. Pape say to Mark, "Hasn't it struck you that but for the sins of your youth you might be doing stunts round these good-looking hills?") His Frenchmen, I believe, are not much better. Even Ford's minor English characters in even second-rate books are often superb, but *The Last Post* was in more than one sense the Last of England. Thereafter, his novels were addressed to American readers, brought out first by American publishers, and—with a single exception—they were about American women and men. They are probably best left forgotten.

By 1928 the war was ten years over. History had slipped away, and with it had passed Ford's subject of subjects. Marie Léonie with her garrulous circularity was an indication of things to come. In his final novels he seems to have been no longer able to hold history and the individual affair in a single vision as he had in *The Good Soldier* and *Parade's End*. Instead, things are allowed to fall apart, and we are left in a whirl of technique and inaccurate slang. Perhaps too by this time he had reached an age when individual affairs no longer particularly interested him. But the past still interested him, and it is pleasing to recall that in his late works of nonfiction such as *The March of Literature* Ford showed no signs of faltering.

A Bibliographical Check List

Novels by Ford

The Shifting of the Fire. London: T. Fisher Unwin, 1892.
The Inheritors. With Joseph Conrad. London: William Heinemann, 1901.
Romance. With Joseph Conrad. London: Smith, Elder, 1903.
The Benefactor. London: Brown, Langham, 1905.
The Fifth Queen. London: Alston Rivers, 1906.
Privy Seal. London: Alston Rivers, 1907.
An English Girl. London: Methuen, 1907.
The Fifth Queen Crowned. London: Eveleigh Nash, 1908.
Mr. Apollo. London: Methuen, 1908.
The "Half Moon." London: Eveleigh Nash, 1909.
A Call. London: Chatto & Windus, 1910.
The Portrait. London: Methuen, 1910.
The Simple Life Limited ("By Daniel Chaucer"). London: John Lane, 1911.
Ladies Whose Bright Eyes. London: Constable, 1911; Philadelphia: J. B. Lippincott, 1935 (revised).
The New Humpty-Dumpty ("By Daniel Chaucer"). London: John Lane, 1912.
The Panel. London: Constable, 1912. (Published in the U. S. as *Ring for Nancy.* Indianapolis: Bobbs-Merrill, 1913.)
Mr. Fleight. London: Howard Latimer, 1913.
The Young Lovell. London: Chatto & Windus, 1913.
The Good Soldier. London: John Lane, 1915; New York: Albert & Charles Boni, 1927; New York: Alfred A. Knopf, 1951.
The Marsden Case. London: Duckworth, 1923.
The Nature of a Crime. With Joseph Conrad. London: Duckworth, 1924; New York: Doubleday Page, 1924.
Some Do Not. London: Duckworth, 1924; New York: Thomas Seltzer, 1924.

No More Parades. London: Duckworth, 1925; New York: Albert & Charles Boni, 1925.

A Man Could Stand Up. London: Duckworth, 1926; New York: Albert & Charles Boni, 1926.

The Last Post. New York: The Literary Guild of America, 1928; London: Duckworth, 1928.

A Little Less Than Gods. London: Duckworth, 1928; New York: The Viking Press, 1928.

No Enemy. New York: The Macaulay Company, 1929.

When the Wicked Man. New York: Horace Liveright, 1931; London: Jonathan Cape, 1932.

The Rash Act. New York: Ray Long & Richard R. Smith, 1933; London: Jonathan Cape, 1933.

Henry for Hugh. Philadelphia: J. B. Lippincott, 1934.

Vive Le Roy. Philadelphia: J. B. Lippincott, 1936; London: George Allen and Unwin, 1937.

Parade's End. New York: Alfred A. Knopf, 1950.

Other Books by Ford Mentioned or Cited

The Brown Owl: A Fairy Story. London: T. Fisher Unwin, 1892.

Ford Madox Brown: A Record of His Life and Work. London: Longmans, Green, 1896.

The Spirit of the People: An Analysis of the English Mind. London: Alston Rivers, 1907.

England and the English: An Interpretation. New York: McClure, Phillips, 1907. (Contains *The Soul of London, The Heart of the Country,* and *The Spirit of the People.*)

The Critical Attitude. London: Duckworth, 1911.

Memories and Impressions: A Study in Atmospheres. New York: Harper & Brothers, 1911. (Published in England as *Ancient Lights.* London: Chapman and Hall, 1911.)

Henry James: A Critical Study. London: Martin Secker, 1913; New York: Octagon Books, 1964.

Collected Poems. London: Max Goschen, 1914.

Between St. Dennis and St. George: A Sketch of Three Civilisations. London: Hodder and Stoughton, 1915.

Thus to Revisit: Some Reminiscences. London: Chapman & Hall, 1921; New York: E. P. Dutton, 1921.

Women and Men. Paris: Three Mountains Press, 1923.

Mister Bosphorus and the Muses. London: Duckworth, 1923.

Joseph Conrad: A Personal Remembrance. London: Duckworth, 1924; Boston: Little, Brown, 1924.

A Mirror to France. London: Duckworth, 1926.

The English Novel: From the Earliest Days to the Death of Conrad. Philadelphia: J. B. Lippincott, 1929; London: Constable, 1930.

Return to Yesterday. London: Victor Gollancz, 1931; New York: Horace Liveright, 1932.

It Was the Nightingale. Philadelphia: J. B. Lippincott, 1933; London: William Heinemann, 1934.

Portraits from Life. Boston: Houghton Mifflin, 1937; Chicago: Henry Reguery, 1960. (Published in England as *Mightier than the Sword*. London: George Allen & Unwin, 1938.)

The March of Literature: From Confucius' Day to Our Own. New York: The Dial Press, 1938; London: George Allen and Unwin, 1939.

Books about Ford

Hunt, Violet. *The Flurried Years*. London: Hurst and Blackett, 1926. (Published in the U.S. as *I Have This to Say*. New York: Boni and Liveright, 1926.)

Bowen, Stella. *Drawn from Life: Reminiscences*. London: Collins, 1941.

Goldring, Douglas. *South Lodge: Reminiscences of Violet Hunt, Ford Madox Ford and the* ENGLISH REVIEW *Circle*. London: Constable, 1943.

Goldring, Douglas. *The Last Pre-Raphaelite: The Life and Writings of Ford Madox Ford*. London: MacDonald, 1948. (Published in the U.S. as *Trained for Genius*. New York: E. P. Dutton, 1949.)

Young, Kenneth. *Ford Madox Ford*. London: Longmans, Green, 1956.

Cassell, Richard A. *Ford Madox Ford: A Study of His Novels*. Baltimore: Johns Hopkins University Press, 1961.

Wiley, Paul L. *Novelist of Three Worlds: Ford Madox Ford*. Syracuse: University of Syracuse Press, 1962.

Meixner, John A. *Ford Madox Ford's Novels: A Critical Study*. Minneapolis: University of Minnesota Press, 1962.

Harvey, David Dow. *Ford Madox Ford, 1873–1939: A Bibliography of Works and Criticism*. Princeton: Princeton University Press, 1962.

Ohmann, Carol. *Ford Madox Ford: From Apprentice to Craftsman*. Middletown, Connecticut: Wesleyan University Press, 1964.

Index